WeightWatchers®
The complete
kitchen

Tamsin Burnett-Hall has been a cookery writer for 15 years. Regularly creating and testing good food means she really understands the importance of eating healthily and watching her weight. This is her seventh cookbook for Weight Watchers. She lives with her family in Colchester.

First published in Great Britain by Simon & Schuster UK Ltd, 2012
This edition first published in 2015 by Simon & Schuster UK Ltd
A CBS COMPANY

13579108642

Simon & Schuster UK Ltd, 222 Gray's Inn Road, London WC1X 8HB
www.simonandschuster.co.uk
Simon & Schuster Australia, Sydney
Simon & Schuster India, New Delhi

A CIP catalogue record for this book is available from the British Library.
ISBN 978-1-47114-150-8

Photography: Steve Baxter *Prop styling:* Rachel Jukes
Food styling: Kim Morphew *Hand Model:* Anna Hitchin *Design and typesetting:* Jane Humphrey
Printed and bound in China

Pictured on the back cover: Perfect Pancakes, page 26

WeightWatchers®
The complete
kitchen

Tamsin Burnett-Hall

SIMON &
SCHUSTER

London · New York · Sydney · Toronto · New Delhi

A CBS COMPANY

If you would like to find out more about Weight Watchers and the **ProPoints** Plan, please visit: www.weightwatchers.co.uk

V This symbol denotes a vegetarian recipe and assumes that, where relevant, free range eggs, vegetarian cheese, vegetarian virtually fat-free fromage frais, vegetarian low fat crème fraîche and vegetarian low fat yogurts are used. Virtually fat-free fromage frais, low fat crème fraîche and low fat yogurts may contain traces of gelatine so they are not always vegetarian. Please check the labels.

✱ This symbol denotes a dish that can be frozen. Unless otherwise stated, you can freeze the finished dish for up to 3 months. Defrost thoroughly and reheat until the dish is piping hot throughout.

Recipe notes

Egg size: Medium unless otherwise stated.

Raw eggs: Only the freshest eggs should be used. Pregnant women, the elderly and children should avoid recipes with eggs which are not fully cooked or raw.

All fruits and vegetables: Medium unless otherwise stated.

Chocolate: Use chocolate with a minimum of 70% cocoa solids.

Low fat spread: Where a recipe states to use a low fat spread, a light spread with a fat content of no less than 38% should be used.

Stock: Stock cubes should be used in the recipes, unless otherwise stated. Prepare them according to the packet instructions, unless directed otherwise.

Microwaves: Microwave timings are for an 850 watt microwave oven.

Recipe timings: These are approximate and meant to be guidelines. Please note that the preparation time includes all the steps up to and following the main cooking time(s), including making any other recipes.

Low fat soft cheese: Where a recipe states to use low fat soft cheese, a soft cheese with a fat content of less than 5% should be used.

ProPoints *values*: Should you require the **ProPoints** values for any of the recipes within this book, you can call Customer Services on 0845 345 1500 and we will provide you with the relevant information on a recipe-by-recipe basis. Please allow 28 days.

contents

Cooking know how

Cooking the Weight Watchers way

Learning to cook the Weight Watchers way may mean that you need to change some of the basic methods you use to cook your food. Grilling, steaming or baking are easy ways to cook because they don't require any additional fat. You'll find that a non-stick frying pan will become an essential part of your kitchen, because with it you can cook with little or no added fat. It works well with calorie controlled cooking spray, or adding a precise measured amount of oil. You may be surprised to find you can cook with as little as ½ a teaspoon of oil.

Cooking with stock: you can place chopped or sliced onion in a lidded pan with a little stock instead of oil and cook for about 5 minutes. The onion will become soft and sweet.

Steam-frying: stir-frying can be adapted to steam-frying (especially for vegetables); start by stir-frying in calorie controlled cooking spray until lightly browned then add 2–3 tablespoons of water, cover with a lid and cook until the water has evaporated and the stir-fry ingredients are tender, adding more water if needed.

Steaming: steaming might sound daunting if you've not cooked this way before, but it simply involves cooking food (particularly vegetables) over a small amount of boiling water until tender. Whilst you may wish to buy an electric steamer, you can achieve the same result by using a sieve or colander set inside a lidded saucepan, with water in the base. You don't need to buy lots of expensive equipment to cook healthily.

Portion sizes: instead of guessing at portion sizes, use measuring spoons, scales and a measuring jug to ensure accuracy. It's easy to overestimate portion sizes when judging by eye, which will mean that you are probably consuming more calories than you think.

General cooking tips

Plan ahead: deciding on your meals in advance makes it easier to stick to your healthy eating plan. It also saves money as you only buy the ingredients that you will actually use.

Be prepared: start by reading through your chosen recipe fully to ensure you have all the ingredients and so you know what to expect and what order to do things in.

Get organised: get your ingredients and cooking equipment out before you start cooking.
– If you need boiling water at any stage of the recipe, put the kettle on before you start cooking so that it is at the ready.

Browning meat: if you want to brown something, make sure the pan is hot before you add your ingredient(s).
– Don't overcrowd the pan when browning (especially for meat and poultry), as it will cook in its own juices rather than brown (and may well become tough).
– Don't move meat too soon when browning; it needs time to form a crust and will then release itself from the pan without effort.

Tidy as you go: have a sink full of hot soapy water so that you can wash up as you go, then you won't be left with a whole heap of dirty dishes after your meal.

Batch cooking: think about batch-cooking. Make a double quantity so that you can chill or freeze half for another meal. It's barely any extra effort, but double the reward.

Food preparation tips

Onions: slice off the top, leave the root attached and cut in half, through the root. Discard the skin. The root will hold the onion together as you slice or chop it.

Shallots: for easy-to-peel shallots, place in a bowl and cover with boiling water for 1–2 minutes to loosen the skins.

Garlic: to peel garlic, trim the base off each garlic clove, place on a chopping board and press down with the flat side of a large kitchen knife (or use a wooden spoon) to loosen the skin.

Chillies: halve the chillies lengthways, scrape out the seeds and the white pithy membranes using a small spoon. Slice or chop the chillies as required.

Tomatoes: to peel tomatoes, first cut a shallow cross in the base of each tomato. Place in a bowl and cover with boiling water for 1 minute. Drain immediately and refresh in cold water. The skin should lift away easily.

Mushrooms: there's no need to peel or to wash cultivated mushrooms, simply brush down with kitchen paper if needed.

Butternut squash: use a swivel-headed peeler to easily peel the tough skin from the squash. Cut off the bulbous end, slice in half and scoop out the seeds and pith with a spoon.

Peppers: cut in half through the stem then remove and discard the seeds and white pithy sections.

Leeks: top and tail then cut vertically from the top, almost to the base. Wash under the tap, fanning out the layers to release trapped dirt. Shake dry before slicing.

Mangoes: for sliced mango, don't peel, simply slice the cheeks away from the slightly flattened central stone, and cut into slices. For mango chunks, simply slice the cheeks from either side of the stone and score a diamond pattern through the flesh (but not through the skin). Use both thumbs to push up the centre of each mango cheek, to make a mango 'hedgehog'. Slice chunks of mango away from the skin. In both cases, don't forget to cut the rest of the mango flesh away from the stone before discarding it.

Breadcrumbs: simply tear the bread into rough pieces then whizz to crumbs in a food processor or liquidiser. You can even grate the bread into crumbs although this takes longer. Tip the breadcrumbs into a plastic freezer bag and label with the date. Store in the freezer. The crumbs can be used straight from frozen.

Meat and poultry: there's no need to wash raw meat and poultry. Cooking raw meat and poultry properly is the only way to be sure that these germs won't harm you. Simply pat the raw meat or poultry dry with kitchen paper if needed, and remove any visible fat.

Organising your kitchen

To cook efficiently, it helps to get yourself organised. You may want to start with a good clear-out of your kitchen cupboards, getting rid of out-of-date ingredients (or those foods you know you will find too tempting) and arrange things so that healthy food choices are always to hand. Have a sort through your cooking equipment and storecupboard too. Then turn to these helpful lists of equipment and storecupboard basics to ensure you have what you need to get the most out of your kitchen.

Equipment list

Essential utensils
Measuring spoons
Wooden spoons
Non-stick turner
Slotted spoon
Whisk (preferably non-stick)
Vegetable peeler (preferably a U-shaped
    peeler with swivel-blade)
Can opener
Potato masher
Small paring knife, larger general
    purpose kitchen knife, bread knife
Box grater

Useful utensils
Kitchen scissors
Garlic crusher
Ladle
Spatula (scraper)
Hand-held fine grater for zesting and for
    grating Parmesan

Essential pans
Non-stick saucepans: sizes small, medium
    and large, with thick bases to conduct
    heat evenly, heatproof handles and,
    ideally, see-through lids
Non-stick frying pans: one about 28 cm in
    diameter for general use, one 18–20 cm
    diameter for omelettes and pancakes.
    Choose pans with a thick base to avoid
    distortion and to conduct heat evenly,
    ideally with an ovenproof handle too.
Casserole (flameproof and ovenproof),
    approx 22 cm in diameter, 3.5 litres
    capacity

Useful pans
Griddle pan (non-stick)
Steamer basket insert (or can improvise
    with sieve or colander set in a pan)

Essential baking dishes/tins
Non-stick cake tins: 18 cm sponge tins
    (pair), 20 cm deep springform or loose-
    based tin, 12-hole muffin tin, rectangular
    baking tin 19 x 23 cm
Baking dishes: 20 cm square dish + 25 cm
    square dish, 23 x 30 cm rectangular dish
Non-stick baking tray (ideally one large flat
    tray plus one rectangular tray with sides)
Deep roasting tin, approx 22 x 30 cm
Non-stick loaf tin, approx 23.5 x 13 cm

Essential miscellaneous equipment
Chopping board (including a separate one
    for raw meat/fish)
Measuring jug, preferably clear for accuracy
Kitchen timer (or use oven timer)
Sieve
Mixing bowls (stacking)
Cooking liners/baking parchment (plus foil
    and cling film)

Useful miscellaneous equipment
Colander
Wire cooling rack (or can
    improvise with grill rack)
Food storage containers

Oil spray bottle
Oven thermometer (hangs from oven shelf
    and checks accuracy of oven thermostat
    and temperature dial)

Essential electrical
Hand-held blender or liquidiser
Scales (preferably Weight Watchers)

Useful electical
Electric hand mixer (or can use hand whisk
    but will take longer)
Food processor and/or mini chopper

Storecupboard list

Baking and sweet ingredients

Baking powder and bicarbonate of soda
Cocoa powder
Dried fruits: sultanas, apricots, cranberries
Fast action dried yeast
Flour: plain, self-raising and cornflour
Honey
Porridge oats
Sugar: caster, soft light brown
Vanilla extract

Basic cooking ingredients

Black peppercorns (in a mill)
Calorie controlled cooking spray
Fresh root ginger
Garlic
Olive oil
Onions
Salt (preferably sea salt or low sodium)
Stock cubes or powder

Canned goods

Canned fruit in natural juice (e.g. peaches,
    pineapple, apricots, pears)

Canned pulses in water (e.g. chick peas,
    kidney beans, cannellini beans)
Canned vegetables (e.g. sweetcorn)
Chopped tomatoes
Reduced fat coconut milk
Tomato purée
Tuna in brine or spring water

Dairy

0% fat Greek yogurt
Eggs
Half fat mature cheese
Low fat soft cheese (less than 5% fat)
Low fat spread (with a fat content lower
    than 38%)
Parmesan cheese
Skimmed milk
Virtually fat-free fromage frais and yogurt

Frozen

Frozen berries
Frozen vegetables e.g. peas, sweetcorn
Low fat ice cream

Pasta, rice, noodles etc.

Dried lentils (e.g. red, Puy lentils)
Dried noodles (Oriental)
Dried pasta (preferably wholegrain)
Dried rice (e.g. long grain white and brown
    basmati, risotto)
Plain couscous

Sauces, condiments, spices and herbs

Balsamic vinegar
Fat-free salad dressing
Herbs: bay leaves, dried mint, mixed herbs,
    rosemary, sage, thyme
Lemon juice
Light mayonnaise
Mustard
Soy sauce
Spices: chilli powder, ground cinnamon,
    ground cumin, medium curry powder,
    ground ginger, ground mixed spice,
    nutmeg
Thai sweet chilli sauce

Roasting chart

Meat	Result	Cooking time per kg (pound)	Oven temperature
CHICKEN		45 mins per kg (20 mins per lb) + 20 mins extra	Gas Mark 5/190°C/fan oven 170°C
BEEF	*Rare*	45 mins per kg (20 mins per lb) + 20 mins extra	Gas Mark 5/190°C/fan oven 170°C
BEEF	*Medium*	55 mins per kg (25 mins per lb) + 20 mins extra	Gas Mark 5/190°C/fan oven 170°C
BEEF	*Well done*	65 mins per kg (30 mins per lb) + 30 mins extra	Gas Mark 5/190°C/fan oven 170°C
PORK		65 mins per kg (30 mins per lb) + 30 mins extra	Gas Mark 4/180°C/fan oven 160°C
LAMB	*Medium-rare*	45 mins per kg (20 mins per lb) + 20 mins extra	Gas Mark 5/190°C/fan oven 170°C
LAMB	*Medium*	55 mins per kg (25 mins per lb) + 25 mins extra	Gas Mark 5/190°C/fan oven 170°C
LAMB	*Well done*	65 mins per kg (30 mins per lb) + 30 mins extra	Gas Mark 5/190°C/fan oven 170°C
DUCK		45 mins per kg (20 mins per lb) + 20 mins extra	Gas Mark 6/200°C/fan oven 180°C
TURKEY	*Under 4 kg (inc. boneless joints)*	20 mins per kg (10 mins per lb) + 70 mins extra	Gas Mark 5/190°C/fan oven 170°C
TURKEY	*Over 4 kg*	20 mins per kg (10 mins per lb) + 90 mins extra	Gas Mark 5/190°C/fan oven 170°C

Managing your kitchen

Shopping tips

Planning menus: planning your week's menu and shopping list is one of the key tools for sustained healthy eating. Once you've decided on your chosen meals, use your recipe book(s) to make a shopping list. If you divide your list into sections, your shopping trip should be faster and more organised, for example fruit and vegetables; dairy; meat and fish; frozen; storecupboard. Don't forget to check use-by dates on perishable foods, buying the items with the longest shelf life.

Cooking seasonally: cook as seasonally as you are able to; for one thing you will enjoy the variety, rather than cooking the same meals week-in, week-out. Buying foods in season also means that they are at their peak flavour-wise, and they should also be cheaper than at other times of year, because there is a glut of them. See opposite for a guide to some seasonal foods.

What makes a cut of meat lean?

Lean cuts have the least visible fat on them, and tend to come from the inner parts of the animal. As on our bodies, animals generally store fat under the skin and this translates to having a strip of fat along the edge of a chop, steak or slice of bacon. At home, this can easily be cut away to make the cut leaner.

The naturally lean and most tender cuts of all are the fillet and loin cuts, which aren't particularly active muscle areas. Large areas of muscle, such as the leg, also tend to be quite lean. Active areas such as the shoulder of an animal tend to be marbled throughout with fat, even when the exterior layer of visible fat is removed. If you can keep these differences in mind, it may help when you next need to come up with an instant substitution at the supermarket.

Food storage tips

Many perishable foods need to be kept in the fridge, below 5°C to stop harmful bacteria growing on them.

- Raw chicken (and other poultry), meats and fish should be kept well covered at the bottom of the fridge, to prevent dripping on to other foods resulting in cross-contamination.
- Cooked food (including cooked meats such as ham, or leftovers) should be kept covered on any shelf above raw products, as should dairy products.
- Vegetables stay fresher for longer in the 'crisper' drawers at the bottom of the fridge.

Leftovers: should be covered, stored in the fridge and eaten within two days, except for rice which should be eaten within 24 hours (it must be cooled and refrigerated quickly after cooking), as it can contain a particularly tough type of bacteria that can survive heating. Always reheat leftovers until steaming hot, and do not reheat more than once. If you only use part of the contents of a can, decant into a container and cover before refrigerating.

Packs of mushrooms: covered in plastic wrap, mushrooms can quickly go slimy in the fridge, as condensation forms on the wrap. To avoid this, simply make a couple of holes in the wrapper, or remove the plastic completely and cover the mushrooms with a sheet of kitchen paper.

Packets of fresh herbs: often go limp very quickly. To store cut fresh herbs for longer you can either stand them in a glass of water in the fridge, or wrap them in damp kitchen paper before replacing in their plastic packet.

Bread: don't keep bread in the fridge; this actually dries it out faster. For best results, store bread in an airtight bag on the counter or in a breadbin.

Salad: unlike most salad ingredients which stay crisp and fresh in the fridge, tomatoes and avocados should be kept at room temperature. Tomatoes develop a soft and mushy texture if refrigerated, while if they are kept in a dish on the countertop (or windowsill or vegetable rack) they will continue to ripen and develop in flavour. The flesh of avocados goes black in the fridge, so you should also keep these out of the fridge.

Enjoying seasonal highlights

Month	Fruit	Vegetables	Meat and fish	Last chance for
JANUARY	forced rhubarb, citrus (especially blood oranges and Seville oranges)	cabbage, Brussels sprouts, parsnips, celeriac, swede, turnips, Jerusalem artichoke, kale		pomegranates and cranberries
FEBRUARY	forced rhubarb, citrus fruits	purple sprouting broccoli, leeks, chard, leafy greens and root vegetables		Seville oranges
MARCH	blood oranges and other citrus, rhubarb	young carrots, purple sprouting broccoli, spinach, cabbages and root veg	sea trout and wild salmon	
APRIL	Alphonso mango, gooseberries, rhubarb	Jersey royals, spring onions, watercress, fresh herbs	spring lamb, salmon, crab	mussels and oysters
MAY	Alphonso mango, apricots, gooseberries, nectarines, early strawberries	asparagus, globe artichokes, radishes, rocket, salad leaves, new potatoes	spring lamb, salmon, crab, lemon sole, sardines	Jersey Royals
JUNE	strawberries, raspberries, redcurrants, gooseberries, greengages, nectarines, apricots, cherries	French and broad beans, courgettes, peas and mangetout, salad vegetables, new potatoes	lamb, English veal, crab, fish of all types	asparagus
JULY	apricots, cherries, greengages, nectarines, peaches, blueberries, raspberries, strawberries, figs, melons	aubergines, fennel, tomatoes, peppers, chillies, beans of all types, peas, courgettes and salads	English veal, lamb, crab, mackerel, salmon, sardines, sea bass	blackcurrants, redcurrants, cherries
AUGUST	apples, apricots, damsons, grapes, figs, nectarines, melons, peaches, plums	aubergines, peppers, tomatoes, sweetcorn, marrow, summer salads, beetroot, peas, beans, courgettes	game birds, scallops	strawberries, raspberries, crab
SEPTEMBER	blackberries, apples, pears, plums, figs	squash and pumpkins, cabbage, cauliflower, new season root vegetables	mussels, oysters, scallops and clams, game birds, venison, autumn lamb	sweetcorn, beans, peas, courgettes, summer salads, tomatoes
OCTOBER	apples, pears, quince, sloes, walnuts	wild mushrooms, pumpkins, broccoli, kale, cabbage, celeriac, carrots, potatoes		
NOVEMBER	apples, cranberries, clementines and satsumas, dates, pomegranate, chestnuts	Brussels sprouts, parsnips, pumpkin, swede, celery, Jerusalem artichokes, leafy greens		
DECEMBER	cranberries, citrus fruits, chestnuts	Brussels sprouts, celeriac, cabbage, kale, Jerusalem artichokes, parsnips and other root vegetables	turkey, goose, venison, mussels, oysters and scallops	

CHAPTER : 1

Kitchen basics

The fresh-tasting flavours of a home-made dressing are hard to beat. It's also the simplest thing to prepare – just measure and mix.

This is the perfect dressing for a creamy potato salad or for any time that you are looking for a lighter version of a mayonnaise-based sauce.

Vinaigrette dressing

Calories per serving 70
5 minutes in total
V Makes 4 tablespoons

1 teaspoon Dijon mustard
1 tablespoon white wine vinegar
2 tablespoons extra virgin olive oil
1 teaspoon caster sugar
freshly ground black pepper

1 Place all the ingredients in a small screw-top jar or small bowl with 1 tablespoon of water and shake or whisk vigorously until mixed together well. The dressing will keep in the fridge for 1 week. Allow 1 tablespoon per serving.

Try this

For a balsamic dressing: substitute the basic ingredients with 1 teaspoon grain mustard, 1 tablespoon balsamic vinegar, 2 tablespoons walnut oil, 1 teaspoon clear honey and 1 tablespoon cold water.

For a honey and lemon dressing: substitute the basic ingredients with 1 teaspoon grain mustard, 1 tablespoon lemon juice, 2 tablespoons extra virgin olive oil, 1 teaspoon clear honey and 1 tablespoon cold water.

Creamy dressing

Calories per serving 30
5 minutes in total
V Serves 4

100 g (3½ oz) low fat plain yogurt
60 g (2 oz) low fat mayonnaise
¼ teaspoon Dijon mustard
1 tablespoon snipped fresh chives
freshly ground black pepper

1 Put the yogurt, mayonnaise and mustard in a small bowl and stir together until smooth. Mix in the chives and season to taste with black pepper. Allow 1 tablespoon per serving.

Try this

For a Thousand Island dressing: omit the chives from the basic recipe above, then flavour with 1 tablespoon tomato ketchup, a few drops of Worcestershire sauce, 1 tablespoon sweet chilli sauce and a squeeze of lime juice.

A fabulously fragrant dressing that is lovely on a noodle-based salad (see Oriental Beef Noodle Salad on page 56). It can also be drizzled over grilled chicken or fish to liven them up.

Fat-free Oriental dressing

Calories per serving 30
5 minutes in total
V Serves 1

juice of ½ a lime
1 heaped teaspoon clear honey
¼ teaspoon red chilli, de-seeded and diced
½ teaspoon fresh lemongrass, chopped very finely
1 tablespoon chopped fresh coriander

1 Mix the lime juice and honey together until blended, then stir in the chilli, lemongrass and coriander. This dressing is at its best when freshly made, but it will keep for 1 day in the fridge. Store well covered.

An indispensable, quick recipe for making your own stock from scratch. It has a lovely fresh flavour and makes a fantastic base for home-made soup.

Vegetable stock

Calories per serving 16
5 minutes preparation
25 minutes cooking
V ✳ Makes 1.2 litres (2 pints)

1 onion, chopped roughly
1 leek, sliced
2 celery sticks, chopped roughly
2 carrots, peeled and chopped roughly
2 tomatoes, chopped roughly
a few parsley stalks

1 Place all the ingredients in a large saucepan and add 1.5 litres (2¾ pints) cold water.
2 Bring to the boil, skim the surface and then simmer gently for 20 minutes.
3 Strain the stock before use. If you are going to store the stock in the fridge or freezer, cool completely beforehand.

✳ Freezer tip
Stock can be frozen very successfully, but it's bulky to freeze in its liquid state. Instead, try boiling the strained stock rapidly until it has reduced to at least a quarter of its original volume. Freeze in an ice cube tray then turn out into a plastic bag for storage once frozen. Place a few cubes of frozen stock in a measuring jug and add boiling water to make the stock up to the volume required in your recipe.

As the name implies, this is a terrific all-round gravy that goes with everything from the Sunday roast (including vegetarian versions) to sausage and mash, to mid-week grilled chops with steamed new potatoes. This recipe uses chopped onion, but if you prefer a smooth gravy, simply pass it through a sieve before serving. Try making a double batch and then freeze what's left over to use another time and make things easier for the next meal.

Goes-with-everything gravy

Calories per serving 55

10 minutes preparation

10 minutes cooking

V ✱ Serves 4

calorie controlled cooking spray

1 onion, chopped finely

1 tablespoon plain flour

1 teaspoon tomato purée

1 tablespoon soy sauce

4 tablespoons red wine

400 ml (14 fl oz) vegetable stock

a pinch of dried thyme

1 Spray a lidded saucepan with the cooking spray, add the onion and cook for 6–7 minutes over a medium heat until the onion is softened and browned, adding a splash of water if the onion starts to stick.

2 Add the flour and tomato purée and cook for 1 minute, stirring. Remove the pan from the heat and add the soy sauce and wine, mixing until smooth.

3 Gradually add the stock, stirring as you go. Add the thyme then return the pan to the heat. Bring the sauce to the boil then reduce the heat, cover and simmer for 10 minutes. If you prefer a thicker gravy, remove the lid and continue to simmer until it's as thick as you like it. Serve the hot gravy in a warmed jug.

Cook's tip

Taking the pan out of direct contact with the heat reduces the likelihood of lumps forming.

Try this

Replace the red wine with dry cider, if you prefer (fantastic with sausages), or with port, for a really rich flavour.

If you don't want to use alcohol, simply increase the amount of stock to 450 ml (16 fl oz).

This is a marvellous curry sauce and the perfect recipe for making a large quantity of sauce and then freezing what's left over to use later. To make your curry complete, simply add your chosen extra ingredients (see ideas below), and simmer until cooked through.

Curry sauce

Calories per serving 61
5 minutes preparation
25 minutes cooking
V ❋ Serves 8

1 large onion, chopped finely
600 ml (20 fl oz) vegetable stock
1½ tablespoons medium curry powder
2 garlic cloves, crushed
2.5 cm (1 inch) fresh root ginger, grated
2 x 400 g cans chopped tomatoes
50 g (1¾ oz) mango chutney

1 Place the onion in a large lidded saucepan with 100 ml (3½ fl oz) of the stock. Cook, covered, for 5 minutes until starting to soften.
2 Stir in the curry powder, garlic and ginger and cook, stirring, for 1–2 minutes to bring out the flavour.
3 Tip in the tomatoes and add the mango chutney plus the rest of the stock. Bring to the boil, cover and simmer for 15 minutes.
4 Depending on your preference, the sauce can be kept as it is, slightly chunky, or it can be blended until smooth using a hand-held blender.
5 Divide the sauce into portions; cool before freezing spare portions in labelled sealed containers.

Try this
For a prawn and pepper curry: for each portion of curry sauce, first stir-fry half a sliced yellow pepper in calorie controlled cooking spray until starting to colour. Add the curry sauce and 100 g (3½ oz) cooked, peeled tiger prawns and simmer for 2–3 minutes until piping hot.

For a chicken curry: for each portion of curry sauce, add 1 x 150 g (5½ oz) skinless chicken breast, diced, and simmer in the sauce for 8–10 minutes until the chicken is cooked through. Add 1 heaped tablespoon frozen peas a couple of minutes before the end of the cooking time.

For a butternut squash, chick pea and spinach curry: dice 150 g (5½ oz) peeled butternut squash, spray with calorie controlled cooking spray and roast in the oven at Gas Mark 6/200°C/fan oven 180°C for 20 minutes or until tender. Add to the curry sauce with 50 g (1¾ oz) young leaf spinach and 2 heaped tablespoons of canned chick peas, drained. Simmer for 3–4 minutes.

This is a very useful and simple sauce to liven up a stir-fry.

It's always good to have a simple tomato sauce recipe handy. These flavourings add depth, while a little caster sugar cuts down on the acidity of canned tomatoes.

Oriental stir-fry sauce

Calories per serving 51
5 minutes in total
V Serves 2

½ tablespoon cornflour
2 tablespoons soy sauce
1 tablespoon dry sherry
1 heaped teaspoon clear honey
1 cm (½ inch) fresh root ginger, grated
1 garlic clove, crushed
½ red chilli, de-seeded and diced

1 Blend the cornflour with 2 tablespoons of cold water in a small bowl. Add the soy sauce, sherry and honey. Stir until blended then mix in the ginger, garlic and chilli. Add a further 150 ml (5 fl oz) cold water. Your sauce is now ready to use in a stir-fry (see *Try this* below).

Cook's tip
If the sauce has been sitting for a while as you prepare your stir-fry ingredients, make sure that you give it a quick stir before adding to your wok as the cornflour tends to sink to the bottom of the bowl.

Try this
For an Oriental stir-fry: stir-fry your chosen ingredients in calorie controlled cooking spray until tender and cooked through. Give the sauce a final mix in its bowl to blend the ingredients and then add to your wok or frying pan. Toss everything together for 1–2 minutes until the sauce thickens and coats your ingredients.

Speedy tomato sauce

Calories per serving 28
5 minutes preparation
10 minutes cooking
V ✳ Serves 4

400 g can chopped tomatoes
1 garlic clove, crushed
½ teaspoon grated lemon zest
¼ teaspoon mixed dried herbs
1 teaspoon caster sugar
freshly ground black pepper

1 Place all the ingredients in a lidded saucepan and bring to the boil. Cover and then simmer for 10 minutes, stirring once or twice, then use in your chosen recipe.

Cook's tip
This versatile sauce can be made in larger batches and frozen, once cooled, in sealed plastic containers.

Try this
For a spicy tomato sauce: add half a chopped chilli or a pinch of dried chilli flakes.

This is an endlessly versatile sauce and especially good in recipes such as lasagne or fish pie or Cauliflower Cheese on page 106, and pictured opposite. You can add all sorts of flavourings to the sauce, such as parsley which makes a lovely sauce for fish, or cheese, as suggested in the variation below.

Simple white sauce

Calories per serving 112
10 minutes in total
V ✳ Serves 4

40 g (1½ oz) low fat spread
40 g (1½ oz) plain flour
450 ml (16 fl oz) skimmed milk
1 bay leaf

1 Put all the ingredients into a non-stick saucepan. The mixture will look very unpromising, with lumps of flour and low fat spread, but it will come together beautifully in the next step.

2 Place over a medium-high heat and cook, stirring all the time. As the sauce heats, the flour and low fat spread will blend to give a smooth sauce.

3 Continue stirring until the sauce thickens and comes to the boil then reduce the heat and simmer for 2 minutes.

4 Remove the bay leaf before using in your chosen recipe.

Cook's tip

You can also use sauce flour to make a fat-free white sauce. Using the same quantities as the basic recipe above, but omitting the low fat spread, blend a little of the milk with the sauce flour in a non-stick saucepan, stirring (off the heat) to make a smooth paste. Gradually add the remaining milk, stirring again, then pop the bay leaf in the pan and add a quarter of a vegetable stock cube (or ½ teaspoon vegetable bouillon powder). Place on a medium heat and bring the sauce to the boil, stirring frequently until thickened. Simmer the sauce for 2 minutes, and remove the bay leaf before use.

Try this

For a cheese sauce: add ½ teaspoon Dijon mustard, 25 g (1 oz) freshly grated vegetarian hard Italian cheese and 40 g (1½ oz) grated half fat mature cheese to the cooked white sauce, stirring until melted.

How to fix

If your sauce does become lumpy (sometimes this can happen if it's been left alone on the heat as it thickens), you can usually rescue it by whisking well with a balloon whisk to break up the lumps. Make sure you use a non-metallic whisk so you don't damage the non-stick coating of the pan, or alternatively, transfer the sauce to a bowl before using a metal whisk. If the sauce is still lumpy, you can press it through a sieve into a clean saucepan and then cook for a couple of minutes more.

If you love bread sauce with turkey at Christmas, try this easy version, which is also fabulous next to a simple roast chicken instead of gravy. For a mid-week meal, wrap a 125 g (4½ oz) skinless chicken breast in a rasher of lean back bacon, and bake in the oven for 20 minutes before serving with the bread sauce.

Bread sauce

Calories per serving 52

5 minutes preparation + 30 minutes
    standing

15 minutes cooking

V ❄ excluding crisp crumb topping

Serves 6

300 ml (10 fl oz) skimmed milk

2 shallots, sliced

1 bay leaf

75 g (2¾ oz) fresh breadcrumbs

1 tablespoon half fat crème fraîche

freshly grated nutmeg

freshly ground black pepper

1   Place the milk in a lidded non-stick saucepan with the shallots and bay leaf. Bring to a simmer and cook for 1 minute. Remove from the heat, cover the pan and leave for 30 minutes for the flavours to develop.

2   Strain the milk and discard the shallots and bay leaf. Add 60 g (2 oz) of the breadcrumbs to the milk and cook over a very gentle heat for 10 minutes, stirring occasionally, to allow the breadcrumbs to swell and thicken the sauce.

3   Meanwhile, toast the rest of the breadcrumbs in a small frying pan until golden brown and crisp. Set aside.

4   When ready to serve, stir the crème fraîche into the bread sauce and season generously with the nutmeg and pepper to taste. Serve sprinkled with the crispy crumbs.

Make ahead

The bread sauce can be made ahead and reheated, but don't add the crispy crumb topping until you are ready to serve.

A fruit crumble is one of the ultimate comfort puddings. Here's a quick recipe for a foolproof crumble topping to use on top of your favourite fruit, or try one of the variations below.

Perfect crumble topping

Calories per serving 166

5 minutes preparation

V ✳ Serves 4

75 g (2¾ oz) plain flour

40 g (1½ oz) low fat spread

40 g (1½ oz) soft light brown sugar

25 g (1 oz) porridge oats

1 Sift the flour into a mixing bowl then use your fingertips to rub the low fat spread in until the mixture looks like breadcrumbs. Stir in the sugar and porridge oats; the crumble topping is now ready.

2 Pour the crumble topping over your prepared fruit and lightly press it down.

3 Bake in a preheated oven at Gas Mark 4/180°C/fan oven 160°C for 25–30 minutes until the crumble is golden brown and crisp on top, with the juices from the fruit starting to bubble up around the edges.

Cook's tip

You can make a large batch of crumble topping and store portions in the freezer in plastic food bags, ready to knock up a quick crumble. There's no need to defrost the crumble topping before use.

Try this

For an apple crumble: peel, core and slice 800 g (1 lb 11 oz) cooking apples into a lidded saucepan and add 1 teaspoon ground cinnamon, 3 tablespoons water and 40 g (1½ oz) caster sugar. Cover and cook for 6–7 minutes until the apples are starting to soften and break down. Tip into a baking dish, press the crumble topping on top of the fruit and bake as above.

For a no-effort crumble: drain 2 x 410 g cans pear slices in natural juice and then tip the pear slices into a baking dish, add 150 g (5½ oz) frozen raspberries and top with the crumble topping and bake as above.

Shortcrust pastry is usually made with plain flour, but this version works better with self-raising flour as it gives the pastry a lighter, more crumbly texture.

Shortcrust pastry

Calories per serving 133

5 minutes preparation

   + 30 minutes chilling

V ✳ Makes 250 g (Serves 6)

150 g (5½ oz) self-raising flour
75 g (2¾ oz) low fat spread
a pinch of salt

1 Sift the flour into a mixing bowl. Add the low fat spread then use an ordinary table knife to start to cut the spread into smaller pieces, mixing them into the flour as you go.

2 Next, using your fingertips, rub the ingredients together until the mixture looks like breadcrumbs. Lift your fingers up above the bowl as you rub them to incorporate as much air as possible.

3 Stir in a small pinch of salt then gradually add enough cold water to bring the pastry together, without making it at all sticky – you'll probably need about 2 tablespoons in total, but stop adding water as soon as the pastry starts to hold together in lumps (adding too much water makes the pastry tough). The mixture will still look quite dry at this stage, but gently bring it together by hand and you will find that the pastry should stick together in a ball, leaving the bowl clean.

4 Wrap the pastry in cling film or pop it in a plastic food bag and chill it in the fridge for 30 minutes before rolling out.

Cook's tip

Chilling the pastry before rolling it out has two purposes: first, to allow the pastry to 'relax' (this means that the gluten in the flour can develop evenly), reducing shrinkage when rolled out and, secondly to firm up the fat and make rolling out easier since the pastry is too soft at first.

Try this

You can flavour your pastry by adding lemon or orange zest for a sweet pie, or perhaps a pinch of dried herbs for a savoury pie or tart.

A luscious dessert sauce that can be served in a variety of ways.

This 'cream' is ideal for desserts where you would normally use whipped cream. It's lovely as a topping for fruit or in a filo pasty case with summer berries.

Hot chocolate sauce

Calories per serving 76

5 minutes preparation

V Serves 6

2 heaped teaspoons cocoa powder

1 tablespoon cornflour

50 g (1¾ oz) caster sugar

25 g (1 oz) plain chocolate, chopped

1 tablespoon half fat crème fraîche

1 Mix the cocoa powder, cornflour and sugar together in a non-stick saucepan. Measure out 300 ml (10 fl oz) cold water in a jug then add 4 tablespoons to the saucepan to make a paste then gradually stir in the rest of the water.

2 Place the pan on a medium heat and bring the sauce to the boil, stirring as it thickens.

3 Simmer for 2 minutes, then remove from the heat and stir in the chocolate and crème fraîche. Stir until blended with the sauce then serve, divided between six.

Try this

You could drizzle a serving of the sauce over a 60 g (2 oz) scoop of low fat vanilla ice cream or pour it over sliced bananas or drained canned pears in natural juice. It could also become a dipping sauce for chopped fresh fruit such as strawberries, grapes and pineapple.

Sweet 'cream' filling

Calories per serving 55

5 minutes in total

V Serves 4

150 g (5½ oz) 0% fat Greek yogurt

50 g (1¾ oz) low fat soft cheese

3 teaspoons icing sugar

½ teaspoon vanilla extract

1 Place all the ingredients together in a bowl and beat until smooth. Chill, covered, in the fridge until ready to serve.

Cook's tip

Be sure to use natural vanilla extract rather than vanilla essence or flavouring, which are both synthetic reproductions and don't have as good a flavour.

Try this

You can flavour the 'cream' with other ingredients to complement whatever you are serving it with: try using a ½ teaspoon of grated orange, lemon or lime zest.

Try serving one portion of this delectable creamy topping in a meringue nest, adding a handful of raspberries or canned peach slices in natural juice for a luxurious pudding that takes only a matter of minutes.

Making pancakes from scratch is far easier than you may think. The batter can be whisked up in just a couple of minutes, and as long as you have a good non-stick frying pan there shouldn't be any problems with the pancakes sticking as you cook them. Use a non-stick spatula to flip the pancakes over, to avoid any kitchen calamities.

Perfect pancakes

Calories per serving 65

20 minutes in total

V ✳ Makes 8 pancakes

100 g (3½ oz) plain flour

a pinch of salt

1 egg

200 ml (7 fl oz) skimmed milk mixed
    with 5 tablespoons cold water

calorie controlled cooking spray

1 Sift the flour and salt into a mixing bowl. Make a well in the centre and add the egg. Pour in a little of the milk-water mixture and begin to stir, gradually drawing in the flour as you go. Add the rest of the milk-water mixture, a bit at a time, stirring until you have a smooth batter. Pour into a jug. This will make it easier to pour the batter into the frying pan.

2 To make the pancakes, heat a 18 cm (7 inch) non-stick frying pan (omelette size) over a medium heat. Lightly spray with the cooking spray and then pour in enough batter to coat the base of the pan. Tilt the pan to spread the batter around evenly. Cook for about 1 minute until the underside of the pancake is set and golden brown. Slide a non-stick turner or wooden spatula under the pancake and flip it over. Cook the second side for about 30 seconds, or until spotted with brown.

3 Slide out on to a plate, and cook the rest of the batter in the same way to make a total of eight pancakes, spraying the pan with a little more cooking spray before you make each one. Place a strip of baking parchment between each pancake on the plate to keep them separate. Cover with a clean tea towel to keep warm.

Cook's tip

Using part milk, part water in the batter results in a lighter pancake.

How to fix

If the batter is lumpy, simply whizz it in a liquidiser or with a hand blender until smooth.

Home-made bread is simply wonderful, and it's incredibly easy to make, as well as economical. If you know you'll be tempted by freshly baked bread, slice it once cool and then freeze, sealed in a plastic food bag. You can then toast the slices straight from frozen to enjoy home-baked bread whenever you fancy.

Brilliant bread

Calories per serving 96

10 minutes preparation + rising

30 minutes cooking

V ✳ Makes 16 slices

450 g (1 lb) strong white bread flour

1 teaspoon (½ x 15 g sachet) fast action dried yeast (see Glossary on page 250 about storing leftover yeast)

1 teaspoon caster sugar

1 teaspoon salt

300 ml (10 fl oz) tepid water

calorie controlled cooking spray

1   Reserve 2 teaspoons of the flour for kneading and rolling then place the rest in a bowl. Stir in the yeast, sugar and salt. Make a well in the centre. Add most of the tepid water.

2   Use a wooden spoon to bring it all together as a soft but not sticky dough that leaves the bowl clean. Add a little more tepid water if needed.

3   Dust the work surface with 1 teaspoon of the flour and start to knead the dough. Using the heel of your hands, roll the dough away from you, pressing down firmly as you do so, then bring it back towards you and repeat with the other hand, so you are rolling it back and forth with alternate hands. Knead for 3–4 minutes until it feels soft, springy and elastic. If you prod the dough, the indentation should spring back lightly.

4   Return the dough to the mixing bowl and cover with cling film. Leave to rise for 1 hour or until the dough has doubled in size. Preheat the oven to Gas Mark 7/220°C/fan oven 200°C. Lightly grease a 23.5 x 13 cm (9 x 5 inch) non-stick loaf tin with the cooking spray.

5   Knock the dough back by punching it down to deflate it. Tip out on to a surface lightly dusted with the remaining flour and shape into a fat log to fit the tin. Cover the tin with cling film and leave to prove and rise for 30 minutes or until the dough has risen just above the top of the loaf tin. It should feel soft and pillowy if prodded gently.

6   Remove the cling film and bake in the oven for 25 minutes. Tip the loaf out of the tin and return to the oven for 5 minutes, upside down, to crisp the base. The cooked loaf should sound hollow when the base is tapped.

7   Cool completely on a wire rack before slicing so it can be cut evenly.

Try this

For a wholemeal loaf: use half and half wholemeal strong bread flour and white flour.

For bread rolls: in step 5, shape the dough into eight balls and put on a baking tray, lightly greased with cooking spray. Cover with cling film and leave to prove for 20 minutes. Bake for 15 minutes.

Terrific on the side of a saucy curry, these naan breads can also be split and filled with sandwich fillings, as you do with pitta bread.

Naan bread

Calories per serving 199

25 minutes in total + rising

V ✳ Makes 8 naans

425 g (15 oz) plain flour

1 teaspoon (½ x 15 g sachet) fast action
   dried yeast

½ teaspoon salt

150 g (5½ oz) virtually fat-free plain
   yogurt

125 ml (4 fl oz) tepid water

1 teaspoon cumin seeds or black onion
   seeds

1 Reserve 2 tablespoons of the flour for kneading and rolling then place the rest in a bowl. Stir in the yeast and salt and make a well in the centre. Add the yogurt and most of the tepid water.

2 Use a wooden spoon to bring together as a soft but not sticky dough that leaves the bowl clean. Add a little more of the water if needed.

3 Dust the work surface with 1 tablespoon of the flour and start to knead the dough. Using the heel of your hands, roll the ball of dough away from you, pressing down firmly as you do so, then bring it back towards you and repeat with the other hand, so that you are rolling the dough back and forth with alternate hands. Knead for 3–4 minutes until it feels soft, springy and elastic. If you prod the dough, the indentation should spring back lightly.

4 Return the dough to the mixing bowl and cover with cling film. Leave to rise for 1 hour or until the dough has doubled in size. Preheat the oven to Gas Mark 7/220°C/fan oven 200°C and place two baking trays in the oven to preheat.

5 Divide the dough into eight balls and press a few of the seeds on to each ball. Roll each ball out on a lightly floured surface to a rough oval measuring about 10 x 16 cm (4 x 6¼ inches).

6 Place four naans on each of the two preheated baking trays (there is no need to spray them since the flour they were rolled in prevents them from sticking). Bake for 5 minutes until they are puffy and browned in patches. Serve warm, or cool completely before wrapping individually and freezing.

✳ **Freezer tip**

The frozen naans can be reheated directly from the freezer. Sprinkle with a little water and reheat in a preheated oven at Gas Mark 4/180°C/fan oven 160°C for about 5 minutes.

This is a virtually effortless way to get a loaf of bread on the table when you've run out, and don't have time to get to the shops. Wonderful served warm, soda bread is at its best on the day it's made but it also freezes well, or it makes scrumptious toast the day after baking.

Speedy soda bread

Calories per serving 122

5 minutes preparation

20–25 minutes cooking

V ✳ Serves 6

200 g (7 oz) self-raising flour

½ teaspoon bicarbonate of soda

a pinch of salt

100 g (3½ oz) virtually fat-free
  plain yogurt

1 Preheat the oven to Gas Mark 7/220°C/fan oven 200°C. Dust a baking tray with ½ a teaspoon of the flour. Mix the rest of the flour with the bicarbonate of soda and salt in a mixing bowl. Make a well in the centre.

2 Mix the yogurt with 3 tablespoons of cold water and add this to the bowl. Use a table knife to stir and mix to a soft but not sticky dough that leaves the bowl clean. Add a little more water if the mixture is too dry to cling together.

3 Turn the dough out on to the baking tray and pat into a 15 cm (6 inch) round. If you wish, to make cutting easier later, mark the bread into six sections (like cutting a cake) by cutting nearly all the way through the loaf with a kitchen knife.

4 Bake in the oven for 20–25 minutes until risen and golden brown. The soda bread should make a hollow sound when the base is tapped.

5 Cool slightly before eating.

Try this

For cheese and onion soda bread: add 6 chopped spring onions, lightly fried in a little calorie controlled cooking spray, plus 25 g (1 oz) grated half fat Cheddar cheese and ½ teaspoon grain mustard to the soda bread mix, along with the yogurt. Sprinkle an extra 15 g (½ oz) grated half fat Cheddar cheese on top of the loaf before baking.

For sultana soda bread: add 30 g (1¼ oz) sultanas to the soda bread mix with the yogurt.

CHAPTER:2

Breakfasts

Bursting with berry goodness, this smoothie can be whipped up in only a couple of minutes, so it's the perfect choice for a weekday breakfast when you're in a hurry.

Blueberry maple smoothie

Calories per serving 177

5 minutes in total

V Serves 1

75 g (2¾ oz) fresh or frozen blueberries

75 g (2¾ oz) fresh or frozen raspberries

75 g (2¾ oz) 0% fat Greek yogurt

125 ml (4 fl oz) skimmed milk

2 level teaspoons maple syrup

1   Place all the ingredients in a deep container such as a measuring jug that will allow you to use a hand blender without splashing the smoothie all over the kitchen as you blend, or you can use a liquidiser. If you are using fresh berries rather than frozen, you may want to add an ice cube or two in order to chill the mixture.

2   Whizz until smooth and drink immediately.

Try this

For a summer fruits and banana smoothie: replace the blueberries and raspberries with 1 sliced banana and 75 g (2¾ oz) frozen summer fruits. Sweeten with 2 level teaspoons of honey instead of maple syrup.

For a mango and strawberry smoothie: replace the berries with 100 g (3½ oz) roughly chopped fresh strawberries plus the flesh of ½ a peeled mango. Use 125 ml (4 fl oz) freshly squeezed orange juice in place of the skimmed milk.

This crunchy granola mixture can be kept for several weeks in an airtight container in your kitchen cupboard, ready for a quick and delicious breakfast. Simply serve with 140 ml (4½ fl oz) chilled skimmed milk per person and fresh fruit such as raspberries and blueberries. Or enjoy with a 150 g pot of virtually fat-free natural yogurt and a banana per person.

Honey and seed granola

Calories per serving 165

5 minutes preparation

15 minutes cooking

V Serves 10

3 heaped teaspoons clear honey

300 g (11 oz) porridge oats

15 g (½ oz) sunflower seeds

15 g (½ oz) pumpkin seeds

15 g (½ oz) flaked almonds

15 g (½ oz) dried cranberries, chopped

40 g (1½ oz) sultanas

1 Preheat the oven to Gas Mark 6/200°C/fan oven 180°C and line a large baking tray with baking parchment or foil.

2 Gently warm the honey until runny, either in a small saucepan or for 30 seconds in the microwave. Mix the oats, seeds and almonds together in a bowl then add the warmed honey and stir well until everything is evenly coated, and beginning to stick together in small clusters.

3 Spread the mixture out on the lined baking tray and cook in the oven for 12–15 minutes, stirring halfway through, until you have a golden toasted cereal mixture.

4 Leave to cool then stir in the cranberries and sultanas. Store in an airtight container. Each serving weighs 40 g (1½ oz).

Try this

For a fruity yogurt granola pot: to make a coffee-shop style breakfast pot that you can prepare the night before, slice 75 g (2¾ oz) drained canned apricot halves in natural juice (one third of a 411 g can) and place in the bottom of a lidded container. Add 40 g (1½ oz) blueberries and a 150 g pot of virtually fat-free apricot yogurt. Top with 40 g (1½ oz) honey and seed granola and seal the container. If you'd like the granola to stay really crunchy, carry it in a separate small container or a plastic food bag, ready to sprinkle on just before you eat.

If there are some over-ripe bananas sitting in your fruit bowl, put them to good use and turn them into these delicious breakfast muffins. If you're feeling very hungry, enjoy a 150 g pot of virtually fat-free fruit yogurt on the side.

Banana and apricot muesli muffins

Calories per serving 171

15 minutes preparation

20 minutes cooking

V ✳ Makes 12

250 g (9 oz) self-raising flour

1 teaspoon bicarbonate of soda

100 g (3½ oz) caster sugar

2 ripe bananas, mashed

50 g (1¾ oz) low fat spread, melted

150 g (5½ oz) low fat plain yogurt

100 ml (3½ fl oz) skimmed milk

1 egg, beaten

½ x 411 g can apricot halves in natural
    juice, drained and chopped

40 g (1½ oz) muesli

1   Preheat the oven to Gas Mark 6/200°C/fan oven 180°C. Line a 12-hole muffin tin with 12 muffin cases.

2   Sift the flour and bicarbonate of soda into a large mixing bowl then stir in the sugar.

3   In a separate bowl, mix together the mashed bananas, melted low fat spread, yogurt, skimmed milk and egg.

4   Add the wet ingredients to the dry ingredients and stir with a spoon until just combined. Unlike with a regular cake mixture, this should look slightly lumpy, not smooth, and there may still be a few small pockets of flour.

5   Gently stir in the apricots. Make sure that you don't over-mix the muffin batter or the finished muffins will be tough and chewy.

6   Spoon the mixture into the muffin cases, filling each muffin case almost to the top. Sprinkle the tops of the muffins with the muesli then bake in the oven for 20 minutes or until the muffins are risen, golden brown and firm to the touch.

7   Cool in the tin for 5 minutes to allow the muffins to firm up slightly. Remove them and place on a wire rack to finish cooling.

Try this

To make muffins with a tropical flavour twist, replace the canned apricots with a 227 g can of pineapple pieces in natural juice, drained and patted dry on kitchen paper.

✳ **Freezer tip**

Muffins freeze well (and also quickly go stale if stored in a cake tin, so it's best to freeze them instead). Store in a sealed plastic food bag. To defrost, heat in the microwave for about 30 seconds on full power.

A scrumptious brunch dish for sharing on a lazy weekend, with just one pan to wash up afterwards. Relax and enjoy at your leisure, with the weekend papers.

One pan fry-up

Calories per serving 240
20 minutes in total
Serves 2

calorie controlled cooking spray
250 g (9 oz) potatoes, peeled and cut
    into 2 cm (¾ inch) dice
3 bacon medallions, chopped
150 g (5½ oz) chestnut or button
    mushrooms, sliced thickly
2 eggs
freshly ground black pepper

1   Spray a lidded non-stick frying pan lightly with the cooking spray. Stir-fry the potatoes for 3–4 minutes over a high heat until starting to brown at the edges. Season with pepper, add 3 tablespoons of water and cover the pan. Cook, covered, for 5 minutes over a lowish heat, stirring once or twice, until the potatoes are almost cooked through.

2   Remove the lid, add the bacon and increase the heat under the pan to medium. Cook for 2 minutes, then add the mushrooms and cook for a further 2–3 minutes.

3   Make two spaces in the potato mixture and break an egg into each gap. Cover the pan again and cook gently for 2 minutes or until the eggs are cooked to your liking. Serve on warmed plates.

Cook's tip

If your frying pan doesn't have a lid you can improvise with a baking tray or a large plate placed on top, but make sure that you use oven gloves to lift it as it will get hot.

V Try this

Replace the bacon with 50 g (1¾ oz) Quorn Deli Bacon Style Rashers, chopped. They need less cooking than bacon, so add them to the potato and mushroom mixture just before adding the eggs to the pan.

Try this flavourful omelette for a filling breakfast, or as a lovely light lunch or supper. Some grilled tomatoes would be very tasty on the side.

Mushroom and spinach omelette

Calories per serving 262

10 minutes in total

V Serves 1

calorie controlled cooking spray

100 g (3½ oz) mushrooms, sliced thickly

50 g (1¾ oz) baby leaf spinach

25 g (1 oz) low fat soft cheese

a few gratings of nutmeg

2 eggs

freshly ground black pepper

1 Lightly spray a saucepan with the cooking spray, add the mushrooms and fry for 3 minutes until tender. Add a splash of water, if needed, to prevent the mushrooms from sticking to the pan. Stir in the spinach, mixing until it starts to wilt and then add the soft cheese and nutmeg. Remove from the heat and set aside.

2 Have a warm plate to hand, ready for the finished omelette. Place a small non-stick frying pan 18–20 cm (7–8 inches) in diameter over a medium heat. Spray with the cooking spray. Beat the eggs with 1 tablespoon cold water and season with pepper. Pour the mixture into the pan and leave for about 15 seconds or until just beginning to set around the edges. Use a wooden fork or spatula to start to draw the setting edges of the omelette into the centre. Tilt the uncooked egg mixture into the gaps, to give a lightly ruffled appearance.

3 When almost all the free-running egg has set, continue to cook the omelette until the underside is golden brown. The omelette is ready to fill when the top is set, but still looks slightly soft and shiny.

4 Place the filling on one side of the omelette then use a wooden spatula to flip the other half over the filling. Slide out on to the warmed plate and eat immediately.

Cook's tip

Have your filling ready before you start to cook the omelette, as this will only take 2–3 minutes and needs your full attention.

Try this

For a ham and mushroom omelette: cook the mushrooms as above, but omit the spinach and low fat soft cheese. Add the cooked mushrooms to the set omelette, along with a 30 g (1¼ oz) serving of wafer thin ham, cut into strips.

It's best to make this mixed fruit compote the night before you want it, to allow the flavours to mingle and make it even tastier. Keep it in the fridge for up to three days.

Breakfast fruit compote

Calories per serving 207

15 minutes in total + cooling

V Serves 4

411 g can apricots in natural juice,
    drained and juice reserved

3 strips pared lemon zest

¼ teaspoon ground mixed spice

25 g (1 oz) caster sugar

3 ripe but firm pears, peeled, cored
    and cut into wedges

75 g (2¾ oz) ready to eat prunes, halved

To serve

200 g (7 oz) virtually fat-free plain
    fromage frais

2 tablespoons pumpkin seeds

1 Pour 150 ml (5 fl oz) of the reserved apricot juice into a medium saucepan. Add the lemon zest, mixed spice and caster sugar. Bring to a simmer, stirring until the sugar has dissolved.

2 Add the pears and prunes and simmer for about 5 minutes, or until the pears are tender (the exact timing will depend on their ripeness). Remove the pan from the heat and gently stir in the apricots.

3 Leave the fruit to cool, then chill, covered, until ready to serve.

4 To serve, top each serving of compote with 50 g (1¾ oz) fromage frais and half a tablespoon of pumpkin seeds.

Cook's tip

Use a vegetable peeler to pare the zest from a lemon in long strips. Make sure there is no white pith on the underside, as this gives a bitter flavour.

Try this

If you don't like dried fruit, leave out the prunes and increase the pears to four.

This luxurious breakfast dish is an adaptation of the American brunch classic known as Eggs Benedict. Poached eggs may seem like an advanced skill, but with the simple set of instructions below you'll find it quite easy. The key is to use very fresh eggs as the white will set closely around the yolk. Older eggs, which are approaching their 'use by' date, have whites with a much thinner texture that disperses in the cooking liquid.

Poached egg and smoked salmon muffins

Calories per serving 253
20 minutes in total
Serves 4

a small pinch of saffron (or yellow food colouring, see Cheat's tip)
2 tablespoons skimmed milk
100 g (3½ oz) low fat soft cheese
1 tablespoon half fat crème fraîche
¼ teaspoon Dijon mustard
a squeeze of lemon juice
100 g (3½ oz) smoked salmon
2 English muffins, halved
4 very fresh eggs
freshly ground black pepper

1   Get everything ready before you start to poach the eggs. First, make the sauce. Place the saffron (or food colouring) and milk in a small saucepan. Warm gently and stir to start releasing the colour from the saffron. Add the soft cheese, crème fraîche and mustard and mix until smooth. Season with pepper and add a squeeze of lemon juice to taste then set aside.

2   Roughly tear the smoked salmon and divide into four portions, ready to serve, and get the English muffins ready to toast.

3   Bring a deep lidded frying pan (about 4 cm/1½ inches deep) of water to the boil, then reduce the heat until the water is barely simmering. The small bubbles that form on the base of the pan should no longer be rising to the surface. Break each egg in turn into a cup or ramekin then gently tip it into the water, evenly spacing them around the pan. If the eggs aren't completely covered by the water, spoon a little over the top of each one. Cover with a lid and cook for 4 minutes on a low heat.

4   Meanwhile, return the sauce to the hob and heat gently, stirring, but do not allow to boil. Lightly toast the muffins and place half a muffin on each warmed serving plate then top with the smoked salmon.

5   When the poached eggs are ready, lift each one out with a slotted spoon, resting the spoon briefly on kitchen paper to absorb any excess water. Place each egg on top of a muffin and spoon the sauce over the egg. Serve immediately.

Try this
Replace the smoked salmon with a 30 g (1¼ oz) serving of wafer thin ham per person, or with 1 slice of Quorn Deli Style Ham per person.

Cheat's tip
To cut down on cost, you could omit the saffron and add a couple of drops of yellow food colouring instead to give a rich colour to the sauce.

If you're short of time but still fancy a cooked breakfast, this is the way to go.

Speedy breakfast wrap

Calories per serving 258
5 minutes in total
Serves 1

1 egg
35 g (1¼ oz) premium ham, chopped
1 medium flour tortilla
calorie controlled cooking spray
3 cherry tomatoes, chopped
freshly ground black pepper

1 Beat the egg with 1 tablespoon of cold water and season with pepper then stir in the ham.
2 Warm the tortilla for about 15 seconds on each side in a small non-stick frying pan, to make it more flexible. Set aside. Lightly spray the frying pan with the cooking spray and fry the tomatoes for 30–45 seconds until starting to soften.
3 Tip in the ham and egg mixture and cook over a medium heat until almost set. Slide out on to the tortilla wrap, roll up and eat immediately.

V Try this
Replace the ham with Quorn Deli Ham Style Slices.

This speedy cooked breakfast gives you a satisfying start to the day.

Cheese and chive scrambled eggs

Calories per serving 300
5 minutes in total
Serves 1

2 eggs
2 tablespoons skimmed milk
5 g (¼ oz) freshly grated Parmesan cheese
2 teaspoons snipped fresh chives
1 medium slice granary bread
freshly ground black pepper

1 In a non-stick saucepan, beat the eggs and milk together using a non-metallic utensil. Stir in the Parmesan cheese and chives and add pepper to taste. Place over a low heat.
2 Toast the granary bread to your liking.
3 Cook the scrambled eggs gently, stirring constantly until they are softly set. They continue to cook when the heat is turned off, so make sure that you don't overcook them as they will become dry and rubbery. Pile on to the hot toast and eat immediately.

Cook's tip
Cooking slowly over a gentle heat is crucial to ensure a creamy texture.

Try this
For smoked salmon and scrambled eggs: omit the Parmesan cheese and chives from the recipe above, to make plain scrambled eggs. When the scrambled eggs are almost ready, stir in 40 g (1½ oz) smoked salmon, chopped roughly, before piling it on to your hot toast.

This cheerful fruity shake will set you on your way with a spring in your step.

Apricot and buttermilk shake

Calories per serving 147

5 minutes in total

V Serves 2

411 g can apricots in natural juice, drained

284 ml pot buttermilk

3 heaped teaspoons clear honey

2 drops almond extract

a couple of ice cubes (optional)

1 Place the drained apricots in a deep jug with the buttermilk, honey, almond extract and ice cubes, if using.

2 Whizz until smooth using a hand-held blender (or process in a liquidiser). Divide between two glasses and serve immediately.

Cook's tip

If you haven't come across buttermilk before, don't be misled by the name: it is not a high fat buttery milk. Originally, buttermilk was the liquid left over from the butter-making process, but nowadays it is produced by culturing milk, in a similar way to making yogurt, which buttermilk closely resembles. Buttermilk is slightly less sour than yogurt, and a little bit thinner. You can use 250 g (9 oz) virtually fat-free plain yogurt in its place if you prefer.

Crushed banana 'jam' makes a lovely breakfast topping. Swap the crumpets for medium slices of wholemeal toast if you prefer.

Crumpets with banana 'jam'

Calories per serving 184

5 minutes in total

V Serves 2

4 crumpets

2 bananas

a few drops of lemon juice

a small pinch of ground cinnamon

1 Put the crumpets on to toast. Meanwhile, cut half of one banana into thin slices. Mash the rest of the banana with the lemon juice and cinnamon to taste, to make the 'jam'.

2 Spread the banana 'jam' over the crumpets and top with the sliced banana. Enjoy immediately.

A lovely weekend brunch for when you fancy a sweet treat. It's a fantastic combination of little breakfast pancakes, bananas, cool and creamy fromage frais and luscious raspberries.

Sultana drop scones with bananas and raspberry crush

Calories per serving 276

20 minutes in total

V ✳ for drop scones only

Makes 20 drop scones; Serves 4

125 g (4½ oz) self-raising flour

1 egg

150 ml (5 fl oz) skimmed milk

2 heaped teaspoons clear honey

1 tablespoon sultanas

calorie controlled cooking spray

For the raspberry crush

200 g (7 oz) raspberries, fresh or
    frozen (defrosted)

2 heaped teaspoons clear honey

To serve

200 g (7 oz) virtually fat-free
    fromage frais

2 bananas, sliced

1 Sift the flour into a mixing bowl and make a well in the centre. Add the egg and start to mix together, adding the milk until you have a thick, smooth batter. Mix in the honey and sultanas.

2 Place a non-stick frying pan over a medium heat and spray lightly with cooking spray. Drop five separate tablespoons of batter into the pan and cook for 1½ minutes until the underside is golden brown and the top is bubbly and almost set. Flip over and cook for 45–60 seconds until golden brown underneath then transfer to a plate and keep warm, covered with a clean tea towel. Cook the remaining batter in three more batches, to give a total of 20 drop scones.

3 While the drop scones are cooking, crush the raspberries with a fork, and mix with the honey.

4 For each serving, place five drop scones on a plate, top with a quarter of the fromage frais and sliced bananas, then drizzle with the raspberry crush and serve straightaway.

Cook's tip

Honey can be tricky to measure, given its sticky nature. To make life easier, dip the measuring spoon in hot water first and then the honey will slide off easily.

Try this

Serve with a 150 g pot of virtually fat-free fruit yogurt per person for a quick take-to-work breakfast.

✳ Freezer notes

To freeze the drop scones, wrap batches of five in cling film then pop them in a plastic food bag. They can be kept in the freezer for up to 1 month. The drop scones can be defrosted quickly in the microwave (45–60 seconds in a microwave to defrost a batch of five).

CHAPTER : 3

Soups, salads and sandwiches

With its colourful ingredients and a stimulating blend of hot and sour flavours, this aromatic soup not only tastes amazing, it looks great too.

Thai vegetable broth

Calories per serving 65

15 minutes in total

V Serves 1

75 g (2¾ oz) mushrooms, sliced

½ red chilli, de-seeded and sliced

½ stick fresh lemongrass, chopped finely

1 cm (½ inch) fresh root ginger, peeled
    and cut into matchsticks

400 ml (14 fl oz) vegetable stock

1 tablespoon soy sauce

50 g (1¾ oz) baby corn, sliced

40 g (1½ oz) mange tout, halved

juice of ½ a lime

2 tablespoons chopped fresh coriander

1 Place the mushrooms, chilli, lemongrass and ginger in a lidded saucepan with 2 tablespoons of the stock. Cover and cook for 4 minutes.

2 Add the rest of the stock, the soy sauce and baby corn, cover the pan again and cook for 3 minutes. Add the mange tout and cook for a final 2 minutes.

3 Stir the lime juice into the soup, ladle into a bowl and serve scattered with the coriander.

Cook's tip

You're unlikely to use a whole pack of lemongrass in any recipe so chop the remaining lemongrass and store it in a plastic food bag in the freezer, ready to use another time.

Try this

Make the soup into a more substantial supper dish by adding: some cooked noodles (use 40 g/1½ oz dried weight); 100 g (3½ oz) cooked, peeled tiger prawns, or 100 g (3½ oz) cooked skinless chicken breast per serving.

This appetising salad, with its delicious Oriental twist, is another great way to use up leftovers from the Sunday roast. The crucial *Fat-free Oriental Dressing* is easy to make and ready in 5 minutes.

Oriental beef noodle salad

Calories per serving 305

20 minutes in total

Serves 1

50 g (1¾ oz) dried medium egg noodles

1 x recipe Fat-free Oriental Dressing
(see page 15)

60 g (2 oz) cooked lean roast beef,
sliced into strips

1 carrot, peeled and grated coarsely

50 g (1¾ oz) Chinese leaf, shredded

15 g (½ oz) salted peanuts, chopped finely

1   Bring a pan of water to the boil, add the noodles and cook for 3–4 minutes or until tender. Drain and rinse briefly in cold water.

2   Make the Fat-free Oriental Dressing, following the recipe on page 15. Add the dressing to the drained noodles and mix in the beef, carrot and Chinese leaf, tossing well to combine.

3   Scatter the peanuts on top to serve.

Cook's tip

A garnish of finely chopped peanuts is a frequent addition to Thai salads, and adds an extra crunch factor, as well as flavour.

Try this

This recipe is also delicious with 60 g (2 oz) skinless roast chicken, lean roast pork or lean roast lamb per serving.

Alternatively, replace the cooked meat with 100 g (3½ oz) cooked, peeled prawns per serving.

This warming root vegetable soup is especially welcome during the colder months.

Celeriac, leek and potato soup

Calories per serving 153

15 minutes preparation

25 minutes cooking

V ✳ Serves 6

3 leeks, sliced

1.5 litres (2¾ pints) vegetable stock

500 g (1 lb 2 oz) celeriac, peeled and chopped

250 g (9 oz) potatoes, peeled and diced

300 ml (10 fl oz) skimmed milk

6 teaspoons snipped fresh chives

freshly ground black pepper

1 Place the leeks in a large lidded saucepan with 100 ml (3½ fl oz) of the stock. Cover and cook for 5 minutes until starting to soften.

2 Add the celeriac, potatoes, 150 ml (5 fl oz) of the milk and the rest of the stock, plus a seasoning of black pepper. Bring the soup to the boil, cover partially and simmer for 20 minutes until the celeriac and potato are tender.

3 Add the remaining milk to the soup and use a hand-held blender, or transfer to a liquidiser in batches, and blend until smooth. Ladle into warmed bowls and scatter with chives to serve.

Butternut squash makes a fabulous soup as the flesh cooks to a silky smooth texture.

Cumin-spiced squash soup

Calories per serving 112

10 minutes preparation

30 minutes cooking

V ✳ Serves 6

2 onions, chopped

850 ml (1½ pints) vegetable stock

¼ teaspoon chilli flakes

1 tablespoon ground cumin

1 teaspoon ground cinnamon

1 kg (2 lb 4 oz) butternut squash, peeled, de-seeded and chopped

juice of ½ a lemon

1 Place the onions in a large lidded saucepan with 100 ml (3½ fl oz) of the stock. Cover and cook for 5 minutes until softened. Stir in the chilli flakes, ground cumin and cinnamon and cook for 1 minute.

2 Add the squash and the rest of the stock. Cover, bring to the boil and simmer for 15 minutes or until the squash is tender.

3 Using a hand-held blender, or in batches in a liquidiser, blend the soup until smooth. (If using a liquidiser, never fill it more than half full when blending soup.) Add the lemon juice to taste and then serve in warm bowls.

Cheat's tip

Buy ready-prepared butternut squash and frozen chopped onions and there's no preparation at all.

Cooked barley has a slightly nutty flavour. It's ideal for a lunch box salad.

Use left over roast beef from the Sunday roast or simply buy cooked sliced beef from the supermarket if it's easier.

Barley salad with Gorgonzola

Calories per serving 375
10 minutes preparation
30 minutes cooking
V if Gorgonzola is vegetarian
Serves 2

75 g (2¾ oz) dried pearl barley
50 g (1¾ oz) frozen soya beans
1 tablespoon low fat salad dressing
2 ripe pears, peeled, cored and sliced
40 g (1½ oz) Gorgonzola cheese, diced
15 g (½ oz) pecans, toasted and chopped
25 g (1 oz) watercress, torn roughly

1   Bring a large lidded saucepan of water to the boil, add the pearl barley and cook, covered, for 30 minutes or until the barley is tender but still with some bite. Add the soya beans for the last 3–4 minutes of the cooking time.

2   Drain the pearl barley and soya beans and mix with the dressing, pears, Gorgonzola cheese and pecans. Top with the watercress leaves, ready to mix in, as you eat the salad.

Cook's tip
Keen cooks can use 1 tablespoon of the Honey and Lemon Dressing (see *Try this* on page 14) instead of a shop-bought dressing.

Cheat's tip
Replace the pearl barley with a 250 g sachet of pre-cooked Wholewheat Grains (Merchant Gourmet brand).

Tex Mex beef and bean pittas

Calories per serving 293
15 minutes in total
Serves 2

calorie controlled cooking spray
2 shallots, chopped finely
1 garlic clove, crushed
½ teaspoon ground cumin
215 g can kidney beans in water, drained and rinsed
2 tomatoes, chopped roughly
a few shakes of Tabasco Pepper Sauce
2 medium pitta breads
50 g (1¾ oz) Iceberg lettuce, shredded
100 g (3½ oz) lean roast beef, sliced thinly

1   Spray a non-stick frying pan with the cooking spray and cook the shallots and garlic for 2–3 minutes until starting to colour, adding a splash of water if needed to prevent them from sticking to the pan.

2   Add the cumin, kidney beans, tomatoes and 2 tablespoons water and cook for 2 minutes, lightly mashing the beans with a wooden spoon as they cook. Remove from the heat and add Tabasco sauce to taste.

3   Meanwhile, toast the pitta breads and then split open. Spread with the bean mixture and fill with the shredded lettuce and the beef.

Try this
Try 100 g (3½ oz) skinless roast chicken or, for a vegetarian version, replace the beef with 60 g (2 oz) grated half fat mature cheese.

These tasty samosas make a great alternative to sandwiches at lunchtime and are ideal for packing in a lunch box. They take some time to prepare but because they can be frozen before cooking, they're very handy. Simply bake from frozen when you need them. They're tasty with 2 tablespoons of virtually fat-free natural yogurt per person.

Potato and pea samosas

Calories per serving 107

25 minutes preparation + cooling

15 minutes cooking

V ✳ Makes 8

350 g (12 oz) potatoes, peeled and cut
    into 1 cm (½ inch) cubes

1 teaspoon sunflower oil

6 spring onions, sliced

1 cm (½ inch) fresh root ginger,
    peeled and grated

1 teaspoon medium curry powder

½ teaspoon cumin seeds

100 g (3½ oz) frozen peas

2 tablespoons chopped fresh coriander

4 x 45 g (1½ oz) sheets frozen filo pastry,
    measuring 50 x 24 cm
    (20 x 9½ inches), defrosted

calorie controlled cooking spray

1 Preheat the oven to Gas Mark 6/200°C/fan oven 180°C.

2 Bring a pan of water to the boil, add the potatoes, bring back to the boil and cook for 5–6 minutes until tender. Drain well.

3 Meanwhile, heat the oil in a small non-stick frying pan. Add the spring onions, ginger, curry powder and cumin seeds and cook for 1 minute over a medium heat. Add the peas and 2 tablespoons of water. Cook for 1 minute more.

4 Mix the spicy peas with the drained potatoes and coriander then spread out on a plate to cool.

5 Lay a stack of four sheets of filo on a clean working surface and then cut the stack in half lengthways to give eight long strips. Keep the sheets stacked up and cover with a damp tea towel so they don't dry out as you make the samosas. Working with two strips of filo at a time, place an eighth of the filling at the top of each strip. Bring the top left corner down diagonally towards the right hand side to form a triangle and press down lightly so the filling is spread out evenly. Flip the triangle over repeatedly, working down the strip of filo, enclosing the filling inside the filo pastry.

6 Repeat to make a total of eight samosas and place on a non-stick baking tray, lightly coated with cooking spray. Spray the tops of the samosas with a little more of the cooking spray and bake in the oven for 15 minutes until crisp. Serve one samosa per person.

✳ **Freezer hints**

If you're going to freeze the samosas, do this before cooking. Freeze on a baking tray, loosely covered with cling film. Once frozen, wrap individually and store in the freezer for up to 2 months. To bake from frozen, cook for 25 minutes at Gas Mark 4/180°C/fan oven 160°C.

This hearty soup is packed with filling pulses and vegetables to keep you feeling satisfied. If you love the exciting flavours of Tex-Mex food, it's sure to be one of your favourite soups.

Chunky chilli bean soup

Calories per serving 154

10 minutes preparation

30 minutes cooking

V ✳ Serves 6

1 onion, chopped

1.2 litres (2 pints) vegetable stock

3 celery sticks, diced

1 red pepper, de-seeded and diced

1 yellow pepper, de-seeded and diced

2 teaspoons ground cumin

a pinch of dried chilli flakes

2 tablespoons tomato purée

400 g can chopped tomatoes

410 g can kidney beans in water,
    drained and rinsed

198 g can sweetcorn, drained

juice of ½ a lime

3 tablespoons chopped fresh coriander

1   Place the onion in a large lidded saucepan with 100 ml (3½ fl oz) of the stock. Cover and cook for 3 minutes then add the celery and peppers. Cover again and cook for a further 5 minutes.

2   Add the cumin, chilli flakes and tomato purée and cook for 1 minute, stirring, to bring out the flavour, before adding the chopped tomatoes and the rest of the stock. Bring back to the boil and simmer for 10 minutes.

3   Add the kidney beans and sweetcorn to the soup and simmer for 5 minutes. Mix in the lime juice and serve the soup scattered with the coriander.

Cook's tip

Cooking an onion in stock instead of oil at the beginning of a recipe means you can cut out the fat completely but still end up with a sweet and softened onion flavour.

Cheat's tip

To cut down on preparation time, the next time you are chopping onions or peppers, chop a few extra and store each onion or pepper in an individual plastic food bag in the freezer, ready to use in future.

This colourful and filling salad is great for packing up in a lunchbox and taking to work. It's also a great dish to lay out on the table for everyone to help themselves.

Puy lentil, pepper and goat's cheese salad

Calories per serving 237

15 minutes preparation

25 minutes cooking

V Serves 4

1 red pepper

1 yellow pepper

175 g (6 oz) dried Puy lentils, rinsed

2 tablespoons low fat balsamic dressing

4 spring onions, sliced

100 g (3½ oz) goat's cheese, diced

50 g (1¾ oz) wild rocket

1   Preheat the oven to Gas Mark 7/220°C/fan oven 200°C. Place the whole peppers in the oven, directly on the oven shelf, with a foil-lined tray on the shelf below ready to catch the cooking juices - otherwise when the cooking juices drip, they will caramelise and burn on the oven floor. Roast for 15–20 minutes until the skins of the peppers are starting to scorch.

2   Place the peppers in a bowl, cover with cling film and leave to stand for 5–10 minutes, during which time the skins will loosen.

3   Meanwhile bring a saucepan of water to the boil, add the lentils and cook for 20–25 minutes until they are tender.

4   Peel the skins from the peppers and remove the seeds. Cut the flesh of the peppers into short strips.

5   Drain the lentils and mix with the balsamic dressing then stir in the spring onions, peppers and goat's cheese. Gently stir in the rocket leaves just before serving.

Try this

Replace the goat's cheese with 100 g (3½ oz) feta cheese, crumbled.

Cheat's tip

To save time, use two 400 g cans ready-cooked Puy lentils, drained, and replace the fresh peppers with 250 g (9 oz) ready-roasted red peppers in brine, from a jar, cut into strips.

Roasting the peppers brings out their natural sweetness and removing the skin is easy once the pepper has cooled down.

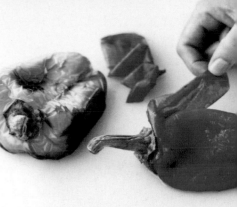

The Quorn tikka filling for these bagels can be served hot or cold so you can make them fresh for lunch at home, or prepare ahead and pack them up for a picnic.

Quorn tikka bagels

Calories per serving 294

10 minutes preparation

10 minutes cooking

V Serves 4

150 g (5½ oz) virtually fat-free plain
    yogurt

2 teaspoons medium curry powder

a squeeze of lemon juice

1 garlic clove, crushed

350 g pack Quorn Chicken Style Pieces

4 Weight Watchers bagels, halved

4 tablespoons low fat mayonnaise

100 g (3½ oz) Iceberg lettuce, shredded

75 g (2¾ oz) cucumber, diced

1   Preheat the grill to high and line a baking tray with foil.

2   To make the tikka pieces, mix together the yogurt, curry powder, lemon juice and garlic until smooth, then stir in the Quorn pieces to coat. Spread out on the foil-lined tray and grill for 10 minutes, stirring two or three times, until the tikka pieces are starting to caramelise at the edges.

3   While the Quorn is cooking, toast the bagels and spread the cut sides with the mayonnaise. Top with the lettuce, cucumber and the tikka pieces.

Try this

You could use a plain 80 g (3 oz) bagel instead.

A seriously scrumptious lunch or light meal, this is a great way to use up a small amount of leftover roast chicken. Great served with a tomato salad, drizzled with a teaspoon of balsamic vinegar.

Chicken, mushroom and spinach tortilla toastie

Calories per serving 260

10 minutes in total

Serves 2

100 g (3½ oz) mushrooms, sliced

25 g (1 oz) low fat soft cheese

2 medium flour tortillas

25 g (1 oz) half fat mature Cheddar, grated

25 g (1 oz) baby leaf spinach

100 g (3½ oz) cooked skinless chicken breast, shredded

freshly ground black pepper

1   Cook the mushrooms with a splash of water in a non-stick frying pan for 3–4 minutes until tender and golden. Season with pepper.

2   Meanwhile, spread the soft cheese on both tortillas. Scatter over the grated cheese, spinach and chicken on one of the tortillas, add the mushrooms and fold the sandwich together with the second tortilla.

3   Wipe the frying pan with kitchen paper then add the tortilla 'sandwich' and cook for 1 minute, pressing down well with a wooden spatula or turner.

4   Place a plate on top of the frying pan and upturn. Slide the tortilla toastie back into the frying pan and cook the second side for a further minute.

5   Cut the tortilla toastie into wedges to serve.

V Try this

For a vegetarian version increase the mushrooms to 150 g (5½ oz) and leave out the chicken.

These pasties are just the thing for a picnic or a packed lunch. They can also be served warm with 150 g (5½ oz) new potatoes per serving, and your favourite steamed green vegetables, for a filling evening meal.

Quorn pasties

Calories per serving 271

55 minutes preparation + 30 minutes
    chilling + cooling

15 minutes cooking

V ✳ Makes 4

1 x Shortcrust Pastry recipe
    (see page 24) + 2 teaspoons plain
    flour, for rolling out

1 small onion, chopped finely

1 carrot, peeled and diced

200 ml (7 fl oz) vegetable stock

150 g (5½ oz) Quorn mince
    (frozen or chilled)

a pinch of dried mixed herbs

1 tablespoon tomato ketchup

40 g (1½ oz) frozen peas

2 teaspoons skimmed milk, to glaze

1 Make up the pastry following the recipe on page 24. Wrap and chill for 30 minutes.

2 Place the onion and carrot in a lidded saucepan with 4 tablespoons of stock and cook, covered, for 6 minutes. Remove the lid and cook for 2 minutes more, until all the liquid has evaporated.

3 Add the Quorn mince, dried herbs, the ketchup and the rest of the stock to the pan. Cover, bring to the boil and simmer uncovered for 5 minutes.

4 Stir in the frozen peas then tip the mixture out on to a plate and leave to cool to room temperature. Preheat the oven to Gas Mark 6/200°C/fan oven 180°C.

5 Divide the pastry into four balls. Dust the work surface lightly with flour and roll each ball out to an 18 cm (7 inches) disc. Place on a flour-dusted baking tray and brush the edges of each circle with a little milk.

6 Spoon a quarter of the cooled mince mixture on to each pastry disc, placing the mince to one side. Fold the pastry over to give a half moon shape. Press the edges together to seal. You can press down using a fork to give a decorative finish, or use your fingers to crimp the edge.

7 Brush the top of each pasty with milk. Bake in the oven for 15 minutes until golden brown and crisp. Serve warm or cool. If cooling them before eating, place on a wire rack so that the pastry stays crisp underneath.

Cook's tip

Don't make the pasties while the filling is still hot or it will melt through the pastry.

Cheat's tip

Use 250 g (9 oz) ready-made shortcrust pastry.

✳ **Freezer hint**

The pasties can be frozen before baking and then baked individually later as needed. Place them on a baking tray, cover with cling film, and put in the freezer. When firm, put in a labelled plastic food bag and seal. Cook from frozen for 25 minutes at Gas Mark 4/180°C/fan oven 160°C.

This aromatic rice salad, studded with colourful nuggets of pistachio, apricot and green beans, tastes even better if you make it the night before. Pack it in a lunchbox with a tightly fitting lid and store in the fridge until ready to eat.

Chicken and pistachio rice salad

Calories per serving 334
10 minutes preparation
20 minutes cooking
Serves 2

75 g (2¾ oz) dried mixed long grain
    and wild rice
75 g (2¾ oz) green beans, chopped
1 tablespoon low fat dressing
15 g (½ oz) shelled unsalted pistachios,
    chopped
40 g (1½ oz) ready to eat dried apricots,
    chopped
2 tablespoons chopped fresh parsley
150 g (5½ oz) cooked skinless chicken
    breast, diced

1   Bring a pan of water to the boil, add the rice and cook for 15 minutes until tender, or according to the packet instructions, adding the green beans for the final 5 minutes of cooking time.

2   Drain the rice and beans and rinse in cold water then shake off the excess water. Mix together with the dressing and stir in the pistachios, apricots, parsley and chicken.

Cook's tips

You can buy the dried mixed long grain and wild rice already mixed together in a packet. The wild rice adds a delicious extra texture to the salad that makes it special.

You could make this recipe with any sort of leftover cooked rice. Use 175 g (6 oz) cooked weight.

Try this

Keen cooks may like to use 1 tablespoon of Vinaigrette Dressing (see page 14) instead of a bought dressing.

For a tuna rice salad: replace the chicken with a drained 185 g can of tuna in spring water.

CHAPTER: 4

Sunday roasts,

leftovers and sides

Roast chicken is a firm favourite for Sunday lunch. Since this chicken is surrounded by a medley of vegetables as it roasts, all you need on the side is a generous serving of your favourite green vegetable, such as runner beans. Any leftover meat can be used in a recipe such as the Russian Chicken, Mushroom and Soured Cream Pie (see page 97).

Roast chicken with herbed cheese stuffing

Calories per serving 401
20 minutes preparation
1¼ hours cooking + 15 minutes resting
Serves 4

1.45 kg (3 lb 3 oz) whole chicken
150 g (5½ oz) low fat soft cheese
2 teaspoons low fat spread
grated zest and juice of ½ a lemon
1 tablespoon chopped fresh thyme
1 tablespoon chopped fresh tarragon
    or 1 teaspoon dried
3 tablespoons chopped fresh parsley
3 leeks, cut into 5 cm (2 inch) chunks
750 g (1 lb 10 oz) butternut squash,
    peeled, de-seeded and diced
calorie controlled cooking spray
300 g (10½ oz) cherry tomatoes

1   Preheat the oven to Gas Mark 5/190°C/fan oven 170°C. Make the stuffing by mixing together the soft cheese, low fat spread, lemon zest and herbs. Gently lift the skin away from the breast meat by slipping your hand in between the skin and the flesh (put on a disposable rubber glove first if you wish). Spoon the stuffing under the skin and smooth it out to form an even layer.

2   Place the chicken in a large roasting tin and cover loosely with foil. Roast for 30 minutes initially.

3   Meanwhile, toss the leeks and butternut squash with a light coating of cooking spray. Remove the foil from the chicken and put the vegetables around the chicken. Roast for 30 minutes, stirring the vegetables halfway through. As the chicken roasts, some of the stuffing will ooze out and mix with the vegetables to form a sauce. After 30 minutes, add the cherry tomatoes and cook for a further 15 minutes or until the chicken is cooked through. The juices should run clear when the thickest part of the leg is pierced with a sharp knife.

4   Let the chicken rest for 15 minutes, loosely covered with foil, before carving and serving 120 g (4½ oz) chicken, without skin, with the vegetables.

Cook's tip
Resting meat after roasting gives the meat time to relax and the juices time to settle within the meat. If you serve it immediately, the roasting juices are lost and the meat may seem dry.

Cheat's tip
To save time, you could use 600 g (1 lb 5 oz) ready-prepared butternut squash.

Melt-in-the-mouth fillet of beef makes a luxurious roast. Serve with 150 g (5½ oz) new potatoes per person, plus steamed baby vegetables. For lunch the next day, you could use up the leftover roast beef in the Oriental Beef Noodle Salad (see page 56).

Roast fillet of beef with red wine sauce

Calories per serving 225

5 minutes preparation

35 minutes cooking + 10 minutes resting

Serves 4

500 g (1 lb 2 oz) piece fillet of beef

calorie controlled cooking spray

3 shallots, chopped finely

100 ml (3½ fl oz) red wine

250 ml (9 fl oz) beef stock

2 level teaspoons cornflour

2 teaspoons redcurrant jelly

freshly ground black pepper

1   Preheat the oven to Gas Mark 7/220°C/fan oven 200°C. Season the beef fillet with black pepper. Heat a non-stick frying pan and spray lightly with the cooking spray. Add the beef and brown for 4 minutes over a high heat, turning to colour on all sides. Transfer the beef to a small roasting tin.

2   Add the shallots to the frying pan and cook for 2–3 minutes until golden. Add the red wine; it will bubble immediately. Pour around the beef in the roasting tin then cover the tin with foil, folding the foil around the edges of the tin to make a tent.

3   Roast the beef in the oven for 20 minutes for rare roast beef, or 30 minutes for medium. Remove the beef to a warm plate, cover loosely with the foil and leave to rest for 10 minutes.

4   Pour the red wine sauce from the roasting tin into a saucepan and add the stock. Bring to the boil. Mix the cornflour with 1 tablespoon of cold water to make a paste, add to the sauce and bring to the boil then add the redcurrant jelly. Stir until the sauce thickens. Slice the beef fillet and serve with the sauce.

Cook's tip
You can buy a beef fillet from the butcher's counter in a supermarket. Even if you don't see it on display, ask the butcher, as they may well have a fillet in the fridge that hasn't yet been sliced into steaks. It's best to request a piece cut from the centre of the fillet rather than from one of the tapered ends, to ensure the same thickness throughout. That way it will cook evenly.

Although the flavours in this roast are inspired by the Mediterranean, the traditional Perfect Roast Potatoes (see page 104) are still fantastic with it. Accompany with some tasty tenderstem broccoli too. Any leftover roast pork is ideal for the Hot and Sour Pork Noodle Soup (see page 96).

Rosemary and fennel roast pork loin

Calories per serving 304
10 minutes preparation
1¼ hours cooking + 15 minutes resting
Serves 4

½ a lemon
1½ tablespoons chopped fresh rosemary
    plus 2 extra sprigs
a few fennel fronds, chopped (optional)
3 garlic cloves, crushed
1 teaspoon olive oil
900 g (2 lb) pork loin joint, trimmed of all
    visible fat
1 fennel bulb, cut into wedges
1 red pepper, cut into wedges
1 yellow pepper, cut into wedges
4 plum tomatoes, quartered
freshly ground black pepper

1   Preheat the oven to Gas Mark 7/220°C/fan oven 200°C.

2   Grate the zest from the lemon and then cut the half lemon into wedges. Place the wedges and rosemary sprigs in the bottom of a roasting tin. Mix the chopped rosemary, fennel fronds (if using), garlic, olive oil and lemon zest together to form a paste, season with black pepper and rub the paste on to the pork. Sit the pork joint on top of the lemon and rosemary in the roasting tin.

3   Roast the pork for 30 minutes then reduce the oven temperature to Gas Mark 4/180°C/fan oven 160°C. Scatter the fennel, peppers and tomatoes around the joint and cook for 40–45 minutes, stirring the vegetables halfway through. To test if the pork is done, the juices should run clear when the thickest section is pierced with a skewer.

4   Remove the pork from the oven, rest it for 15 minutes, and keep the vegetables warm. Discard the rosemary sprigs and lemon wedges. Remove any skin and fat from the pork and carve into slices.

Cook's tip
It's always best to remove a joint from the fridge at least 15–20 minutes before it goes in the oven to give it a chance to come to room temperature. That way, when the meat goes in the oven, the centre won't be fridge-cold and the joint will cook more evenly.

Serve with wedges of roasted butternut squash and heaps of lightly cooked green cabbage. There are no leftovers from this recipe.

Roast lamb with jewelled rice stuffing

Calories per serving 339

20 minutes preparation + 15 minutes resting

1¼ hours cooking

Serves 6

40 g (1½ oz) dried basmati rice

calorie controlled cooking spray

4 spring onions, sliced

15 g (½ oz) shelled pistachios, chopped

15 g (½ oz) dried cranberries, chopped

grated zest and juice of ½ a small orange

750 g (1 lb 10 oz) boneless lamb leg joint

1 Preheat the oven to Gas Mark 5/190°C/fan oven 170°C.

2 Bring a saucepan of water to the boil, add the rice and cook according to the packet instructions until tender then drain and rinse in cold water. Spray a small non-stick frying pan with the cooking spray and fry the spring onions for 1–2 minutes or until softened. Mix with the cooked rice, pistachios, cranberries and orange zest and juice.

3 Remove the bindings from the lamb and unroll it so that it lies flat. Slice through the lamb from the centre towards the sides, but don't cut right through. Open the lamb out to either side (picture it like the jacket on a hardcover book if this helps - see the first step-by-step photo below).

4 Cover the lamb evenly with the stuffing then re-roll the lamb, this time rolling it up like a Swiss roll. Tie with string in three or four places to hold securely. Place the stuffed lamb in a foil-lined roasting tin and cover the joint loosely with a piece of foil.

5 Roast the lamb for 1¼ hours – it will be just pink in the centre; roast for 15 minutes longer if you prefer it cooked all the way through. Rest for 15 minutes before carving.

Cook's tip

Rather than cooking the rice from scratch for this recipe, you can use 100 g (3½ oz) cooked weight of rice left over from the previous night's meal.

While apple sauce is the traditional accompaniment to roast pork (see below for a recipe), why not try glossy glazed pears and carrots instead? You may like to serve it with Goes-with-Everything Gravy (see page 16) too.

Roast pork with glazed pears and carrots

Calories per serving 218
10 minutes preparation
1¾ hours cooking + 15 minutes resting
Serves 6

1.4 kg (3 lb 1 oz) boneless pork leg joint
3 firm pears, halved (any type of pear)
1 tablespoon demerara sugar
750 g (1 lb 10 oz) Chantenay carrots,
    trimmed
2 tablespoons chopped fresh thyme

1 Preheat the oven to Gas Mark 7/220°C/fan oven 200°C. Place the pork joint in a large roasting tin and roast for 15 minutes then reduce the oven temperature to Gas Mark 5/190°C/fan oven 170°C and roast for a further 45 minutes.

2 Meanwhile, use a teaspoon to scoop the cores out of the pear halves. Place the sugar on a small plate and press the cut sides of the pears in the sugar to coat.

3 After 45 minutes, add the carrots to the roasting tin and place the pear halves on top. Scatter the thyme all over then spoon some of the cooking juices over the pears and carrots. Return to the oven and roast for a further 45 minutes or until the pork is cooked through (the juices should run clear when the centre of the joint is pierced with a skewer or small sharp knife), and the pears and carrots are caramelised and tender.

4 Remove the roasting tin from the oven, cover loosely with foil and leave to rest for 15 minutes. Keep the glazed pears and carrots warm.

5 Remove the skin and any fat from the pork and cut the pork into thin slices. Serve 105 g (3½ oz) roast pork per person with the glazed pears and carrots.

Try this

For apple sauce: peel and core two cooking apples then slice them into a lidded saucepan. Add 4 tablespoons of water and 2 tablespoons of sugar. Cover the pan and cook for 7–8 minutes, stirring once or twice, until the apples have collapsed. Serve warm or cold. This quantity makes enough to serve 6 generously.

Flavoured with the classic combination of rosemary and garlic, this is a wonderful way to roast a leg of lamb. It smells simply fabulous as it cooks. This recipe allows for leftover meat which is ideal for the Leftover Lamb Pilaff (see page 98).

Garlic and rosemary roast lamb with roasted roots

Calories per serving 363
20 minutes preparation
1¾ hours cooking + 15 minutes resting
Serves 6

1.75 kg (3 lb 14 oz) whole leg of lamb
    (bone-in)
4 garlic cloves, 2 sliced and 2 crushed
4 fresh rosemary sprigs
6 carrots, peeled and chopped roughly
3 onions, cut into wedges
3 parsnips, peeled and cut into wedges
calorie controlled cooking spray
3 teaspoons redcurrant jelly
grated zest of ½ a lemon
4 cooked beetroot in natural juice,
    drained and cut into wedges

1   Preheat the oven to Gas Mark 5/190°C/fan oven 170°C. Make small incisions all over the leg of lamb with a sharp knife and push a slice of garlic into each one. Place the lamb in a large roasting tin, sitting it on top of two of the rosemary sprigs. Chop the rest of the rosemary finely and rub half of the chopped rosemary all over the lamb. Roast in the oven for 1 hour.

2   In a large bowl, mix the carrots, onion and parsnips with the rest of the chopped rosemary and the crushed garlic. Spray the vegetables lightly with the cooking spray and mix again. Once the initial 1 hour of roasting is up, add the vegetables to the roasting tin, arranging them around the lamb. Roast for a further 30 minutes.

3   Make a glaze for the lamb by mashing the redcurrant jelly with the lemon zest. Spoon this over the lamb. Mix the beetroot in with the other vegetables and roast for 15 minutes. Remove the vegetables to a dish and keep warm. Rest the lamb, loosely covered with foil, for 15 minutes before carving into slices. Serve 120 g (4½ oz) lamb per person, with the roasted root vegetables.

Try this
You can vary the roasted vegetables around the lamb. Instead of parsnips, you could use 600 g (1 lb 5 oz) new potatoes and instead of the beetroot, you could use 3 leeks, cut into chunks, added with the other vegetables.

Oriental butterflied roast chicken

Calories per serving 363

20 minutes preparation

40 minutes cooking + 10 minutes resting

Serves 4

1.45 kg (3 lb 3 oz) whole chicken

2 garlic cloves

2.5 cm (1 inch) fresh root ginger,
    chopped roughly

2 shallots, chopped roughly

2 tablespoons soy sauce

1 tablespoon light brown sugar

juice of ½ a lime

1 red chilli, de-seeded and chopped

600 g (1 lb 5 oz) sweet potatoes, peeled
    and cut into 2 cm (¾ inch) cubes

calorie controlled cooking spray

1 To butterfly the chicken, start by removing any bindings then flip the chicken over so it is resting breast-side down on a chopping board. Using a sturdy pair of kitchen scissors, cut down either side of the backbone, starting at the parson's nose (the pointy nodule by the main cavity). You will easily feel where the backbone is. Simply lift the backbone out and discard. Turn the chicken over and press down firmly to flatten the chicken.

2 Cut off the ends of each leg at the small joint. Next, carefully cut just through the skin, running down the centre of the breast bone. Using kitchen paper to grip the skin, remove it by pulling it first off the breast, and then over and off the legs. Cut the skin around the base of each chicken wing to remove.

3 Make the marinade by placing the garlic, ginger, shallots, soy, sugar and lime juice together in a food processor, or blender, and whizz to make a paste. Stir in half of the chilli. Cut a few slashes in the chicken breast and legs then rub the marinade all over. Place in a large plastic food bag or sealed container and leave to marinate for 30 minutes or overnight in the fridge.

4 Preheat the oven to Gas Mark 5/190°C/fan oven 170°C. Place the chicken in a roasting tin and roast in the lower part of the oven for 40 minutes, or until the juices run clear when pierced with a skewer.

5 While the chicken is in the oven, toss the sweet potatoes with the rest of the chilli. Spray lightly with the cooking spray. Spread out on a baking tray and roast in the oven, above the chicken for 35 minutes, stirring once or twice, until tender and slightly caramelised at the edges.

6 Remove the chicken from the oven and allow to rest, loosely covered with foil, for 10 minutes. Carve and serve 125 g (4½ oz) of chicken per person, with the sweet potatoes.

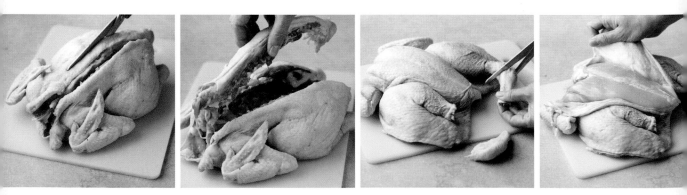

Yorkshire Puddings (see page 107) are just the thing with this classic roast. Use the leftover roast beef for another meal, such as the Quick Vietnamese Curry Noodles (see page 100).

Roast beef with balsamic onions and parsnip purée

Calories per serving 343

20 minutes preparation

1 hour–1¼ hours cooking + 15 minutes resting

Serves 6

1 kg (2 lb 4 oz) joint rolled topside or top rump of beef

freshly ground black pepper

For the balsamic thyme onions

3 red onions, peeled

3 onions, peeled

2 tablespoons balsamic vinegar

2 teaspoons olive oil

1 teaspoon soft light brown sugar

1 tablespoon chopped fresh thyme

1 garlic clove, crushed

For the parsnip purée

6 parsnips, peeled and chopped

4 tablespoons skimmed milk

2 tablespoons half fat crème fraîche

1 Preheat the oven to Gas Mark 5/190°C/fan oven 170°C. Season the beef with black pepper and place in a large roasting tin. Roast in the oven for an initial 30 minutes for rare beef or 45 minutes for medium-well done beef.

2 Cut each onion into six wedges, leaving them attached at the root. Mix the balsamic vinegar, olive oil, sugar, thyme and garlic together in a bowl, add the onions and stir to coat. Set aside.

3 When the initial cooking time is up, add the onion mixture to the roasting tin around the beef and roast for 15 minutes. Turn the onions and add 3 tablespoons of water to the tin to prevent the onions from sticking as they caramelise and roast for a further 15 minutes. Remove the beef from the roasting tin, loosely cover will foil, and leave to rest for 15 minutes before carving. If the onions aren't yet caramelised, return to the oven for a further 5–10 minutes then transfer to a warmed serving dish.

4 While the beef and onions are roasting, bring a lidded saucepan of water to the boil, add the parsnips, bring back to the boil and cook, covered, for 10–15 minutes until they are completely tender. Drain well and leave to steam dry for 1 minute. Add the milk and mash the parsnips until smooth then stir in the crème fraîche. Serve with 105 g (4 oz) beef per person, a portion of the parsnip purée and the balsamic roast onions.

With its lightly spiced mango chutney glaze, this quick roast can easily be served up as a mid-week meal. Serve with baby carrots and broccoli. There are no leftovers for this recipe.

Glazed roast turkey with sesame parsnips

Calories per serving 236

15 minutes preparation

50 minutes cooking + 10 minutes resting

Serves 4

500 g (1 lb 2 oz) skinless boneless
    turkey breast joint

4 parsnips, peeled and cut into chunks

2 teaspoons sesame seeds

½ teaspoon black onion seeds

50 g (1¾ oz) sweet mango chutney

a pinch of ground ginger

grated zest of ½ a lemon

1 teaspoon lemon juice

calorie controlled cooking spray

freshly ground black pepper

1   Preheat the oven to Gas Mark 5/190°C/fan oven 170°C. Place the turkey breast joint in a foil lined roasting tin, season with pepper, cover loosely with foil and roast for 15 minutes initially.

2   Once the turkey is in the oven, bring a saucepan of water to the boil, add the parsnips and bring back to the boil. Cook for 4 minutes or until starting to soften at the edges. Meanwhile, mix the sesame seeds and black onion seeds together in a small bowl. Measure ½ a teaspoon of this mixture into another bowl then mix with the mango chutney, ginger, lemon zest and juice to make the glaze for the turkey.

3   When the parsnips are ready, drain them well. Spray lightly with the cooking spray and sprinkle with the rest of the seed mixture. Toss to coat evenly in the seeds and then add to the roasting tin, around the turkey joint. Remove the foil and return the roasting tin to the oven for 15 minutes.

4   Brush the glaze over the turkey and cook for another 20 minutes or until the juices run clear when pierced with a skewer. If the glaze appears to be burning, cover with the foil again.

5   When cooked, remove the turkey from the oven to rest for 10 minutes, and keep the parsnips warm. Carve the turkey into slices and serve with the parsnips.

Cook's tip

Black onion seeds are sometimes labelled as nigella seeds.

Serve this vegetarian roast with the classic accompaniments of Goes-with-Everything Gravy (see page 16) and Perfect Roast Potatoes (see page 104) plus a variety of vegetables such as carrots and runner beans.

Curried lentil and nut roast

Calories per serving 288

20 minutes preparation

45 minutes cooking

V ✳ Serves 6

200 g (7 oz) dried red lentils, rinsed

1 onion, diced

3 celery sticks, diced

1 red pepper, de-seeded and diced

100 ml (3½ fl oz) vegetable stock

1½ teaspoon medium curry powder

1 garlic clove, crushed

100 g (3½ oz) fresh breadcrumbs

100 g (3½ oz) half fat mature cheese, grated

25 g (1 oz) toasted flaked almonds

2 eggs, beaten

2 tablespoons pumpkin seeds

1 Preheat the oven to Gas Mark 4/180°C/fan oven 160°C and line a 23.5 x 13 cm (9 x 5 inch) non-stick loaf tin with baking parchment.

2 Place the lentils in a lidded saucepan, add cold water to cover and put the lid on the pan. Cook until the lentils begin to split (8–10 minutes). Drain well and place in a large mixing bowl.

3 Meanwhile, in another lidded saucepan, add the onion, celery and red pepper to the vegetable stock and cook for 6 minutes. Remove the lid and cook for 2 minutes longer or until the stock has evaporated then add the curry powder and garlic and cook for 1 minute, stirring, to bring out the flavours.

4 Add the vegetable mixture to the mixing bowl with the lentils then add the breadcrumbs, cheese and almonds. Mix well then stir in the beaten eggs. Spoon the mixture into the prepared loaf tin, level the surface and sprinkle with the pumpkin seeds.

5 Bake in the oven for 45 minutes, or until golden brown and firm. Cool in the tin for 5 minutes before turning out and cutting into slices.

Try this

Any leftover nut roast will be delicious served cold, either with 150 g (5½ oz) hot new potatoes per person, or with a mixed leaf salad and 1 tablespoon of reduced fat coleslaw.

Tuck into this roast Quorn and stuffing tray bake with some Bread Sauce (see page 22). It's also great with steamed spears of tenderstem broccoli on the side.

Quorn roast with herby stuffing balls

Calories per serving 251

20 minutes preparation

35 minutes cooking

V Serves 4

1 butternut squash
   (about 650 g/ 1 lb 8 oz), peeled,
   de-seeded and cut into wedges
calorie controlled cooking spray
8 frozen Quorn fillets
1 heaped teaspoon honey
1 teaspoon grainy mustard
2 teaspoons soy sauce

For the stuffing
1 onion, chopped finely
2 teaspoons chopped fresh sage
1 tablespoon chopped fresh thyme
100 ml (3½ fl oz) vegetable stock
75 g (2¾ oz) fresh breadcrumbs
2 tablespoons chopped fresh parsley
1 teaspoon grated lemon zest
1 egg, beaten

1 Preheat the oven to Gas Mark 6/200°C/fan oven 180°C. Arrange the wedges of butternut squash on a large roasting tray and spray lightly with the cooking spray. Drizzle with 4 tablespoons of water and roast in the oven for 15 minutes.

2 Meanwhile, start to make the stuffing. In a lidded saucepan, add the onion, sage and thyme to the stock and cook for 5 minutes until softened. Remove the lid and cook for 2 minutes to evaporate the liquid. Mix the cooked onion with the breadcrumbs, parsley, lemon zest and beaten egg then shape into eight stuffing balls.

3 After the initial 15 minutes of cooking time for the squash, remove the tray from the oven. Add the stuffing balls and the Quorn fillets to the tray. Mix the honey, mustard and soy sauce together and drizzle over the Quorn fillets. Roast in the oven for 20 minutes until the squash is tender, the stuffing balls are golden brown and the Quorn fillets are piping hot.

Try this

If you'd prefer a meaty main course, replace the Quorn fillets with 4 x 125 g (4½ oz) fresh skinless chicken fillets.

Serve with 150 g (5½ oz) mashed potatoes per person. Leftover ham from this dish is ideal in the Speedy Breakfast Wrap on page 48.

The sharp and spicy flavours of this meal-in-a-bowl soup will get your palate singing. A great way to use up leftover roast meat.

Swedish-style baked ham

Calories per serving 216
10 minutes preparation + 10–15 minutes cooling
1½ hours cooking
Serves 6

750 g (1 lb 10 oz) gammon joint
1 onion, quartered
1 celery stick, chopped roughly
1 bay leaf
6 peppercorns
40 g (1½ oz) fresh breadcrumbs
2 tablespoons grainy mustard
2 heaped teaspoons honey
2 teaspoons chopped fresh dill (optional)

1   Preheat the oven to Gas Mark 4/180°C/fan oven 160°C. Place the gammon joint in a small roasting tin with the onion, celery, bay leaf and peppercorns. Add 1 litre (1¾ pints) cold water. Cover with foil, folding it around the edges of the tin to form a tent.

2   Bake the ham in the oven for 1¼ hours. Remove the cooked ham to a plate and leave to cool for 10–15 minutes. Discard the vegetables and cooking liquid, and increase the oven temperature to Gas Mark 7/220°C/fan oven 200°C.

3   Mix the breadcrumbs, mustard, honey and dill, if using, together to make a stiff paste. Remove any bindings from the ham and trim off any fat or skin. Press the breadcrumb crust on to the ham, return to the roasting tin and cook for a further 15 minutes until the crust is golden brown. Cut the ham into thin slices and serve one sixth of the meat per person.

Hot and sour pork noodle soup

Calories per serving 375
15 minutes in total
Serves 1

60 g (2 oz) dried egg noodles
300 ml (10 fl oz) chicken stock
1 cm (½ inch) fresh root ginger, cut into matchsticks
¼ red chilli, de-seeded and sliced
2 spring onions, sliced
1 tablespoon soy sauce
50 g (1¾ oz) mushrooms, sliced
juice of ½ a lime
25 g (1 oz) baby leaf spinach
75 g (2¾ oz) lean cooked roast pork, sliced into strips

1   Bring a saucepan of water to the boil, add the noodles and cook for 4 minutes until tender, or according to the packet instructions. Drain and rinse briefly in cold water.

2   Meanwhile, place the stock in another saucepan with the ginger, chilli, spring onions, soy sauce and mushrooms. Bring to a simmer and cook for 3 minutes. Add the lime juice.

3   Place the noodles in a deep bowl and top with the spinach leaves and pork. Ladle on the hot mushroom broth and eat straightway.

Try this
Replace the pork with the same amount of skinless cooked chicken, or with 100 g (3½ oz) cooked peeled prawns.

This is a great way to stretch a small amount of leftover cooked chicken to make a hearty family meal. The pie filling is based on a Russian dish called Koulibiac which is typically made from salmon and rice encased in puff pastry but this version uses less pastry. Serve with lightly cooked green cabbage and carrots.

Russian chicken, mushroom and soured cream pie

Calories per serving 338

30 minutes preparation

30 minutes cooking

❊ before baking

Serves 6

125 g (4½ oz) dried basmati rice

3 tablespoons chopped fresh dill

grated zest and juice of ½ a lemon

1 onion, chopped

450 ml (16 fl oz) vegetable stock

350 g (12 oz) mushrooms,
    chopped roughly

40 g (1½ oz) plain flour

150 ml (5 fl oz) reduced fat soured cream

250 g (9 oz) skinless cooked
    chicken breast, diced

200 g (7 oz) puff pastry

2 teaspoons skimmed milk

1 Preheat the oven to Gas Mark 6/200°C/fan oven 180°C. Bring a pan of water to the boil, add the rice, return to the boil and cook for 10 minutes, or according to packet instructions, until the rice is tender. Drain well and mix with the dill and lemon zest then place in the base of a 25 cm (10 inch) square baking dish.

2 While the rice is cooking, place the onion in a large lidded saucepan with 4 tablespoons of the stock. Cover and cook for 5 minutes. Add the mushrooms and a further 4 tablespoons of stock. Cook for another 5 minutes, covered. Stir in the flour and blend in the rest of the stock. Bring to the boil and simmer for 2 minutes then mix in the lemon juice, soured cream and chicken. Spoon on top of the rice in the dish and leave to cool slightly.

3 Roll the pastry out until it is slightly larger than the top of the dish. Dampen the rim of the dish with water then lift the pastry on top, pressing on to the rim of the dish. Brush lightly with milk and bake the pie for 30 minutes until the pastry is risen and golden brown and the filling is bubbling.

Cook's tips

The pie can be made ahead of time and chilled until ready to bake, but make sure that both the rice and the chicken and mushroom filling are cool before you assemble the pie and top it with pastry.

If you prefer, you can make the pies in individual dishes, and freeze some for a later date. Defrost before cooking as above.

V Try this

Omit the cooked chicken and replace with four hard boiled eggs, chopped roughly.

Find some fabulous inspiration with this Middle Eastern pilaff, and see just how delicious leftovers can be. Serve with some cooked fine green beans.

Leftover lamb pilaff

Calories per serving 423
15 minutes preparation
20 minutes cooking
Serves 4

1 onion, chopped
850 ml (1½ pints) vegetable stock
2 courgettes, diced
200 g (7 oz) dried basmati rice
1 teaspoon ground cumin
½ teaspoon ground coriander
40 g (1½ oz) raisins
150 g (5½ oz) frozen peas
175 g (6 oz) leftover lean roast lamb,
    shredded

To serve
3 tablespoons chopped fresh parsley
15 g (½ oz) toasted pine nut kernels
seeds of ½ a pomegranate
150 g (5½ oz) 0% fat Greek yogurt

1 Place the onion in a large lidded saucepan with 100 ml (3½ fl oz) of the stock. Cover and cook for 5 minutes. Remove the lid, stir in the courgettes and cook for 3 minutes.

2 Add the rice, spices and raisins and cook for 1 minute, stirring, to bring out the flavours. Pour in 600 ml (20 fl oz) of the stock. Bring to the boil then stir the rice once. Put the lid back on the pan, reduce the heat to low and cook for 20 minutes, without lifting the lid.

3 About 5 minutes before the end of the pilaff cooking time, bring the rest of the stock to the boil in a small lidded saucepan. Add the peas and return to the boil then mix in the lamb, cover and cook for 3 minutes until piping hot.

4 Drain the lamb and peas then stir into the pilaff. Serve sprinkled with the parsley, pine nut kernels and pomegranate seeds. Spoon some Greek yogurt alongside the pilaff to serve.

Cook's tips
To extract the seeds from the pomegranate, place a sieve over a bowl and squeeze the fruit to loosen the seeds. Pick out any bits of white pith, as it tastes bitter.

If you can't find toasted pine nut kernels, buy untoasted ones and dry-fry them for 1–2 minutes until golden.

Try this
Replace the lamb with the same amount of cooked chicken if you prefer.

These spicy, soupy noodles are a scrumptious way of using up any meat left over from the Sunday roast and are a speedy supper solution.

Quick Vietnamese curry noodles

Calories per serving 387

15 minutes in total

Serves 2

calorie controlled cooking spray

3 shallots, sliced

1 level teaspoon red Thai curry paste

1 teaspoon medium curry powder

200 ml (7 fl oz) reduced fat coconut milk

1 teaspoon soft light brown sugar

200 ml (7 fl oz) vegetable stock

100 g (3½ oz) sugar snap peas, halved

150 g sachet pre-cooked rice noodles

75 g (2¾ oz) beansprouts, rinsed

150 g (5½ oz) cooked lean roast beef, shredded

a squeeze of lime juice

2 tablespoons chopped fresh coriander, to serve

1   Spray a medium non-stick frying pan with the cooking spray and cook the shallots for 2 minutes. Add the curry paste and powder and fry for 1 minute, stirring, to bring out the spice flavours. Pour in the coconut milk which will bubble and thicken slightly.

2   Next add the sugar, stock and sugar snap peas. Cook for 3 minutes then sprinkle in the rice noodles, separating them with your fingers as you do. Mix in the beansprouts and roast beef then heat through for 2–3 minutes until piping hot.

3   Stir in the lime juice to taste and serve scattered with coriander.

Cook's tip

Coconut milk tends to separate into two layers as it stands (a thicker coconut cream forms on the bottom with a lighter coconut milk on the top) so always give a can of coconut milk a good shake to mix everything together evenly before you open the can. Any unused coconut milk can be frozen in an ice cube tray to use another time.

Try this

Instead of the roast beef, you can substitute the same weight of leftover roast pork or roast chicken.

Alternatively, if you don't have any leftovers from a Sunday roast, you can make this recipe with 150 g (5½ oz) cooked peeled tiger prawns.

V For a vegetarian version, omit the meat and add 200 g (7 oz) quartered chestnut mushrooms with the shallots.

This recipe is a great example of how you can turn a little leftover roast chicken into a substantial meal the next day, for very little extra cost. Serve with a mixed leaf salad, dressed with a squeeze of lemon juice.

Zippy chicken and broccoli tagliatelle

Calories per serving 404

10 minutes preparation

10 minutes cooking

Serves 2

125 g (4½ oz) dried tagliatelle

125 g (4½ oz) broccoli, cut into
  small florets

1 teaspoon olive oil

1 garlic clove, sliced

½ red chilli, de-seeded and diced

2 ripe tomatoes, chopped roughly

150 ml (5 fl oz) chicken stock

150 g (5½ oz) skinless cooked chicken
  breast, diced

grated zest of ½ a lemon + 1 teaspoon
  lemon juice

2 tablespoons chopped fresh basil

15 g (½ oz) freshly grated Parmesan
  cheese

1   Bring a saucepan of water to the boil, add the pasta and return to the boil. Cook for 10 minutes until tender or follow the packet instructions. Add the broccoli for the last 3 minutes.

2   Meanwhile, place the oil, garlic and chilli in a saucepan and heat for 1 minute or until the garlic just starts to turn golden. Add the tomatoes and cook for 1 minute so they start to soften then add the stock and chicken and simmer for 3–4 minutes.

3   Drain the pasta and broccoli then mix with the tomato sauce. Add the lemon zest, juice, basil and Parmesan cheese and toss together. Divide between warmed bowls and serve straightaway.

Cook's tip

It's best to keep fresh tomatoes in a bowl on the kitchen counter, not stored in the fridge, which can affect the texture. At room temperature, the flavour can continue to develop and they will ripen in the bowl.

V Try this

Leave out the chicken and it also tastes lovely as a meat-free recipe. Replace the chicken stock with vegetable stock to make it completely vegetarian, and increase the broccoli to 200 g (7 oz).

Roast potatoes are eternally popular and a must-have recipe. The Sunday roast simply isn't the same without them and now you can enjoy this healthy version with all the family.

Perfect roast potatoes

Calories per serving 116

10 minutes preparation

45 minutes cooking

V Serves 6

900 g (2 lb) potatoes (Desirée, King Edward, Rooster or Maris Piper potatoes are best), peeled and cut into chunks

calorie controlled cooking spray

1 teaspoon semolina or dried polenta

1 Preheat the oven to Gas Mark 6/200°C/fan oven 180°C.

2 Bring a lidded saucepan of water to the boil, add the potatoes and bring back to the boil. Cover and cook for 5 minutes or until the edges of the potatoes start to soften.

3 Meanwhile, place a non-stick baking tray in the oven to preheat for 5 minutes.

4 Drain the potatoes well, place the lid on the pan and shake the potatoes to roughen the edges. The rough edges will become lovely and crisp in the oven.

5 Tip the potatoes out on to the preheated baking tray, spray with the cooking spray and sprinkle with the semolina or polenta.

6 Roast the potatoes for 40 minutes, on an upper shelf, turning over halfway through so that all sides become evenly crisp and golden brown.

Cook's tip

If the joint you are roasting needs to cook at a different temperature from this recipe, the potatoes will happily cook at the same temperature as your roast. Just bear in mind that they will cook more quickly at a higher temperature and will need a little longer if the oven temperature is lower than that indicated above. Also, bear in mind that if, for instance, the joint is cooked at Gas Mark 5/190°C/fan oven 170°C, you can increase the oven temperature once the meat is out and resting for 15 minutes before carving, giving the potatoes a chance to crisp up before serving.

Try this

You can also make 'mini roasties' for a mid-week meal. Simply cut the same amount of potatoes into smaller chunks (about 4 cm/1½ inches), allowing 150 g (5½ oz) peeled potatoes per person. Parboil for about 3 minutes, and roast for 25–30 minutes. These are delicious made with a chopped red onion and a sprinkling of chopped fresh rosemary for the last 10 minutes of roasting time.

A little semolina gives these potatoes the crucial crunch factor, which is usually lacking when they are cooked without fat.

This makes a great accompaniment for Sunday roast.

Serve with a medium crusty bread roll, to tear and dip into the lentils.

Cauliflower cheese

Calories per serving 134
20 minutes preparation
20 minutes cooking
Serves 4

1 large cauliflower, separated into florets
1 bay leaf
1 quantity Cheese Sauce recipe (see the variation for
   Simple White Sauce on page 20 or Cheat's tip below)
25 g (1 oz) freshly grated Parmesan cheese

1   Preheat the oven to Gas Mark 6/200°C/fan oven 180°C. Place the cauliflower florets in a steamer, or in a steamer basket set inside a lidded saucepan. Tuck in the bay leaf and add boiling water to the pan. Cover and cook for 10 minutes or until the cauliflower is tender.

2   While the cauliflower is steaming, make the cheese sauce following the recipe on page 20. When the cauliflower is tender, transfer it to a baking dish and pour the sauce all over. Scatter the Parmesan cheese on top.

3   Bake the cauliflower cheese for 20 minutes until bubbling and golden brown.

Cheat's tip
Replace the Cheese Sauce recipe with a 40 g packet of Colman's Cheddar Cheese Sauce Mix made up with 300 ml (10 fl oz) skimmed milk following the pack instructions. Add in step 2 and follow the remaining instructions for the recipe.

Creamy lentils with ham and squash

Calories per serving 309
15 minutes preparation
35 minutes cooking
Serves 4

500 g (1 lb 2 oz) butternut squash,
   peeled, de-seeded and diced
calorie controlled cooking spray
1 onion, chopped
1 carrot, peeled and diced
½ teaspoon ground cinnamon
1 teaspoon ground ginger
600 ml (20 fl oz) vegetable stock
175 g (6 oz) dried puy lentils, rinsed
150 g (5½ oz) lean cooked ham, diced
100 g (3½ oz) low fat soft cheese
3 tablespoons chopped fresh parsley

1   Preheat the oven to Gas Mark 6/200°C/fan oven 180°C. Spread the butternut squash out on a non-stick baking tray and spray lightly with the cooking spray. Roast in the oven for 30 minutes until tender, turning halfway through.

2   Meanwhile, spray a lidded saucepan with the cooking spray. Fry the onion for 3–4 minutes until golden brown. Stir in the carrot, cinnamon and ginger and cook for 30 seconds before adding the stock and lentils. Cover, bring to the boil and simmer for 20 minutes or until the lentils are tender.

3   Stir the ham, soft cheese and roasted squash into the lentils and heat for 3 minutes or until piping hot. Mix in the parsley just before serving.

There's no need to resort to ready-made Yorkshires when it's so quick to whip up a batch of fresh and deliciously crisp ones at home.

Yorkshire puddings

Calories per serving 30

5 minutes preparation

15 minutes cooking

V ✳ Makes 12

60 g (2 oz) plain flour

1 egg

150 ml (5 fl oz) skimmed milk

calorie controlled cooking spray

salt and freshly ground black pepper

1 Preheat the oven to Gas Mark 7/220°C/fan oven 200°C. Place a 12 hole non-stick bun tin in the oven for 5 minutes while you make the batter.

2 Sift the flour into a mixing bowl and make a well in the centre. Break the egg into the well and start to whisk together, drawing flour in from the edges as you whisk around the bowl. As the batter starts to get too thick, gradually incorporate the milk, until you have a thin smooth batter. Season then transfer the batter from the mixing bowl to a jug, for easier pouring – you can re-use the jug that was used to measure the milk.

3 Remove the bun tin from the oven and, working quickly, lightly spray each hole of the tin with the cooking spray. Divide the batter between the moulds in the tin and return to the oven on the top shelf. Bake for 12–15 minutes until the little Yorkshires are well risen, crisp and golden brown.

Cook's tip

It can be tricky to co-ordinate all the elements of your Sunday roast to be ready at the same time, particularly if differing oven temperatures are required. Get ahead of the game by cooking your Yorkshires before the joint even goes in the oven. Remove from the oven and then leave to cool. Simply pop them back in the oven in their tray for 3 minutes to reheat before serving.

✳ Freezer hint

You can freeze any extra Yorkshires in a sealed plastic food bag. They can be reheated from frozen, allowing 4–5 minutes at Gas Mark 6/200°C/fan oven 180°C. Try serving as an easy mid-week meal with two Weight Watchers Premium Pork Sausages and a serving of Goes-with-Everything Gravy on page 16.

CHAPTER : 5

Weekend
suppers

Making your own pizza dough is very simple and also very satisfying. The photographed steps will give you some handy hints if it's the first time you've ever tried it. And you can use the same technique to make the Brilliant Bread recipe (see page 28).

Margherita pizza

Calories per serving 486

25 minutes preparation + 1¼ hours rising

25 minutes cooking

✳ before cooking

Serves 4

200 g (7 oz) strong white bread flour

200 g (7 oz) plain white flour plus
    2 tablespoons extra for kneading

1 teaspoon salt

1 teaspoon (½ x 15 g sachet) fast
    action dried yeast

2 teaspoons olive oil

250 ml (9 fl oz) tepid water

To top the pizzas

1 x Speedy Tomato Sauce recipe
    (see page 19) or see Cheat's tip

150 g (5½ oz) cherry tomatoes, quartered

2 tablespoons shredded fresh basil

125 g pack reduced fat mozzarella
    cheese, drained and diced

25 g (1 oz) freshly grated Parmesan
    cheese

freshly ground black pepper

1 To make the pizza dough, combine both flours in a large mixing bowl with the salt and yeast. Make a well in the centre and add the olive oil and almost all of the tepid water. (The water should feel just warm – if it is too hot, it may kill off the yeast.) Use a table knife or kitchen spoon to bring the liquid and flour together, adding just enough additional tepid water to make a soft dough that comes together without it being sticky, leaving the bowl clean.

2 Dust the work surface with 1 tablespoon of the extra flour and start to knead the dough. Using the heel of your hands, roll the dough away from you, pressing down firmly as you do so, then bring the dough back towards you and repeat with the other hand, so you are rolling the dough back and forth, alternating your hands as you roll. Knead for 3–4 minutes until the dough feels soft, springy and elastic. If you prod the dough, the indentation should spring back lightly.

3 Return the dough to the mixing bowl and cover with cling film. Leave to rise for 1 hour or until it has doubled in size. Preheat the oven to Gas Mark 7/220°C/fan oven 200°C.

4 While the dough is rising, make the Speedy Tomato Sauce, following the recipe on page 10.

5 Punch the dough down to deflate it then divide it into four balls. Dust two baking trays with a little of the remaining flour and use the rest to roll out the dough. For each pizza, shape a ball of dough into a fat disc then use a rolling pin to gently press down on the dough, starting to flatten it in a neat circle before you roll it out. Use the rolling pin to roll out to a 20 cm (8 inch) disc. Transfer to a baking tray. Repeat for the other dough balls.

6 Spread each pizza with a quarter of the sauce then scatter with the cherry tomatoes, basil, mozzarella and Parmesan cheese. Season generously with black pepper and leave to rise for 10–15 minutes.

7 Bake in the oven for 12–15 minutes until the bases are risen, golden brown and crisp at the edges. Swap the trays over after 8–10 minutes.

Cheat's tip

You could use a 300 g jar of ready-made tomato pizza sauce instead of the Speedy Tomato Sauce.

The punchy flavours of this pasta dish are inspired by the delicious cooking of Spain. A peppery watercress, spinach and rocket salad is ideal on the side.

Squid and chorizo pasta

Calories per serving 402

20 minutes in total

Serves 2

125 g (4½ oz) dried pasta (curly pasta
   works well)

60 g (2 oz) diced chorizo

1 red pepper, de-seeded and diced

125 g (4½ oz) sliced squid, rinsed

½ red chilli, de-seeded and diced

2 tomatoes, chopped roughly

½ teaspoon grated lemon zest

2 tablespoons chopped fresh parsley

1   Bring a saucepan of water to the boil, add the pasta and cook for 10 minutes until tender, or according to the packet instructions.

2   Meanwhile, heat a non-stick frying pan, add the chorizo and pepper and fry for 5 minutes over a high heat, stirring occasionally, until starting to brown at the edges.

3   Add the squid and chilli to the pan and cook for 1 minute before adding the tomatoes, lemon zest and 4 tablespoons of pasta cooking water. Cook for 2 minutes more or until the squid is cooked through but still tender.

4   Drain the pasta and toss with the sauce and the parsley. Serve immediately in warmed bowls.

Cook's tip

If you can only buy whole squid rather than ready-prepared sliced squid, you need to pull the tentacles out from the main body sac (these can be used, if you slice off the knobbly end), as well as the clear piece of cartilage from inside the body. Rinse the squid well then slice into rings.

Try this

If squid doesn't appeal, replace with the same weight of raw peeled tiger prawns.

Fatteh is a popular dish in countries such as Syria, Jordan and Lebanon. The name comes from the 'crumbs' of bread that form the foundation of the dish.

Chicken fatteh

Calories per serving 336
20 minutes in total
Serves 2

½ teaspoon mixed spice
a pinch of chilli powder
175 g (6 oz) mini chicken breast fillets
150 g (5½ oz) 0% fat Greek yogurt
1 small garlic clove, crushed
1 teaspoon lemon juice
3 mini pittas, split open
100 ml (3½ fl oz) chicken stock
2 ripe tomatoes, chopped roughly
15 g (½ oz) toasted pine nut kernels
3 tablespoons chopped fresh coriander

1   Combine the mixed spice and chilli powder and rub into the chicken. Heat a non-stick frying pan, add the chicken and dry-fry for 3–4 minutes on each side until cooked through. Transfer to a plate and leave to rest for 5 minutes before slicing.

2   Meanwhile, mix the yogurt with the garlic and half the lemon juice. Toast the pittas until crisp then break up into pieces. Place in the bottom of a shallow serving dish or deep plate. Add the rest of the lemon juice to the stock and drizzle over the pitta pieces.

3   Scatter the tomatoes and half the pine nut kernels over the pitta then spoon over half of the yogurt mixture. Sprinkle with half the coriander then layer with the sliced chicken and the rest of the yogurt, pine nut kernels and coriander. Serve immediately before the pitta loses all of its crispness.

V Try this

For a spicy chick pea fatteh: replace the chicken with a 410 g can of chick peas, drained and rinsed. Pat dry on kitchen paper. Spray a non-stick frying pan with calorie controlled cooking spray, add the chick peas and spices and fry for 3–4 minutes until starting to crisp up. Layer with the fatteh ingredients as above, swapping the chicken stock with vegetable stock.

With a yummy cheese and leek crust on top of the pie, this is classic comfort food. Serve with carrots and broccoli.

Fish pie with cheesy leek topping

Calories per serving 460

35 minutes preparation

25 minutes cooking

✳ before cooking

Serves 4

600 g (1 lb 5 oz) potatoes, peeled
    and chopped roughly

2 eggs

150 g (5½ oz) salmon fillet, with or
    without skin

450 g (1 lb) coley or pollock fillet,
    with or without skin

½ a kettleful of boiling water

2 leeks, sliced

60 ml (2½ fl oz) vegetable stock

40 g (1½ oz) cornflour

450 ml (16 fl oz) skimmed milk plus
    4 tablespoons

1 bay leaf

a squeeze of lemon juice

40 g (1½ oz) half fat mature cheese,
    grated

1   Preheat the oven to Gas Mark 4/180°C/fan oven 160°C.

2   Bring a lidded saucepan of water to the boil, add the potatoes and return to the boil. Cook for 15–18 minutes until tender.

3   Meanwhile, place the eggs in a small saucepan and cover with cold water. Bring to the boil then simmer for 6 minutes. Cool under running water then peel and cut into quarters.

4   Place all the fish in a 20 cm (8 inch) square baking dish, add boiling water to cover the fish then cover the dish with foil. Bake in the oven for 5–6 minutes or until the fish is cooked and starting to flake. Using a slotted turner, remove the fish to a plate then use a couple of forks to break the fish into large flakes, discarding any bones. Wipe the dish clean with kitchen paper, as this will now be used for the pie.

5   Using the saucepan that was previously used to cook the eggs, place the leeks and vegetable stock in the pan, cover with a lid and cook for 8 minutes until softened, then drain.

6   To make the sauce, place the cornflour in a non-stick saucepan with a little of the milk. Stir until smooth then gradually mix in the rest, reserving 4 tablespoons. Add the bay leaf and then bring to the boil, stirring frequently to avoid any lumps. Simmer the sauce for 2 minutes, add the lemon juice and discard the bay leaf.

7   Drain the potatoes and mash with the 4 tablespoons of milk to give a smooth but firm texture.

8   To assemble the fish pie, layer up the flaked fish and hard-boiled eggs in the baking dish. Pour the white sauce evenly over the fish then spoon the mashed potato on top. Spread the leeks in a layer on top of the mash then finish with a scattering of cheese.

9   Place on a baking tray and cook in the oven for 25 minutes or until golden brown and bubbling.

Chermoula is a spicy herb sauce often used to marinate fish or meat before grilling. It's also used as an accompaniment, as in this recipe.

Spicy fishcakes with chermoula sauce

Calories per serving 303

30 minutes preparation + chilling

20 minutes cooking

✳ for uncooked fishcakes only

Serves 4

450 g (1 lb) sweet potatoes, peeled
   and chopped roughly

450 g (1 lb) haddock fillet, with or
   without skin

½ a kettleful of boiling water

1 teaspoon ground cumin

½ red chilli, de-seeded and diced

grated zest and juice of ½ a lemon

6 tablespoons chopped fresh coriander

1 tablespoon plain flour

100 g (3½ oz) fresh breadcrumbs

1 egg, beaten

1 garlic clove, crushed

½ teaspoon smoked paprika

3 tomatoes, diced

1 Bring a saucepan of water to the boil, add the sweet potatoes and return to the boil. Simmer for 10 minutes or until tender.

2 Meanwhile, place the haddock in a frying pan, cover with boiling water and cook gently for 5 minutes or until it flakes easily. With a slotted turner, transfer to a plate. Break into large flakes, discarding any skin or bones.

3 Drain the sweet potatoes and leave to sit for a couple of minutes ('steam-drying' like this prevents the mash from being too wet). Tip into a mixing bowl and mash until smooth. Stir in half of the cumin, half of the chilli, 1 teaspoon of lemon zest and half of the chopped coriander then gently mix in the flaked fish.

4 Shape the mixture into eight fishcakes. Place the flour and breadcrumbs on separate plates and put the beaten egg in a shallow bowl. Taking each fishcake in turn, dip it first in the flour, then in the egg and finally in the breadcrumbs to coat. To avoid crumbing your fingers as well as the fishcakes, use one hand for the flour and egg stages and the other hand to press the breadcrumbs on to the egg-dipped fishcakes. Place the fishcakes on a non-stick baking tray, cover with cling film and chill in the fridge for 30 minutes to give a firmer texture. This will make them hold together better during cooking. Preheat the oven to Gas Mark 6/200°C/fan oven 180°C.

5 Bake the fishcakes for 20 minutes, flipping them after 10 minutes.

6 To make the chermoula sauce that accompanies the fishcakes, lightly toast the remaining ground cumin and the smoked paprika in a dry non-stick frying pan for 30–45 seconds to bring out the flavour. Tip into a bowl and stir in the garlic, remaining chilli and the rest of the lemon zest plus the juice, to make a paste. Stir in the tomatoes and the rest of the coriander plus 2 tablespoons of cold water. Serve with the fishcakes.

Try this

For more traditional fishcakes: replace the sweet potato with the same amount of regular potato, and use smoked haddock instead of fresh haddock. Omit the cumin, chilli and coriander and replace them with 2 tablespoons of chopped fresh parsley plus 1 tablespoon of horseradish sauce. Flour, egg and crumb then cook as per the main recipe.

Instead of grabbing a takeaway, try these lovely lamb pittas with a spicy slaw. They make deliciously fun food.

Saturday night lamb pittas

Calories per serving 408

25 minutes in total

Serves 4

juice of ½ a lemon

1 garlic clove, crushed

1 teaspoon ground cumin

a pinch of hot chilli powder

4 x 100 g (3½ oz) lean lamb leg steaks,
  trimmed of all visible fat

1 onion, sliced thinly

For the spicy slaw

3 tablespoons light mayonnaise

3 tablespoons 0% fat Greek yogurt

2 tablespoons Thai sweet chilli sauce

200 g (7 oz) red cabbage, shredded

2 carrots, peeled and grated coarsely

To serve

4 pitta breads

1   Mix the lemon juice, garlic and spices together in a shallow dish, add the lamb and onion and turn to coat in the mixture. Set aside for 10 minutes while you make the slaw.

2   In a mixing bowl, blend the mayonnaise, yogurt and chilli sauce together then add the cabbage and carrot, mixing together well.

3   Heat a non-stick frying pan over a high heat. Add the lamb steaks, reserving the marinade and cook for 2 minutes on each side (no cooking spray is necessary) or until cooked to your liking – the timings will also vary depending on the thickness of the meat. Remove to a plate and leave to rest, covered loosely with foil.

4   Add the onions and any remaining marinade to the frying pan and stir-fry for 5 minutes until browned, adding a splash of water if the onions start to stick.

5   Slice the lamb thinly and toast the pittas. Slice the pittas open and tuck the lamb and onions into each pitta. Serve with the slaw in the pitta or on the side.

Cheat's tip

You can replace the slaw with 2 tablespoons of reduced calorie coleslaw per person.

Try this

You could replace the lamb steaks with 4 x 100 g (3½ oz) turkey steaks. Cook the steaks for 3–4 minutes on each side to ensure they are completely soaked through.

A classic accompaniment for this Swedish-inspired recipe would be a salad made from diced natural beetroot and tossed with lemon juice and chopped fresh dill.

Salmon burger on rye with horseradish cream

Calories per serving 341

20 minutes in total

❄ for uncooked burgers only

Serves 2

250 g (9 oz) skinless salmon fillet,
    chopped roughly

1 egg white, lightly beaten

25 g (1 oz) fresh breadcrumbs

1 tablespoon capers in brine, rinsed
    and chopped

1 spring onion, chopped

2 slices (40 g/1½ oz) light rye bread

75 g (2¾ oz) 0% fat Greek yogurt

1 tablespoon horseradish sauce

15 g (½ oz) wild rocket

freshly ground black pepper

1   Place the salmon in a food processor and whizz until it is quite finely chopped, but not puréed. If you don't have a processor, then chop as finely as possible by hand, using a large kitchen knife.

2   Mix the salmon together with the egg white, breadcrumbs, capers, spring onion and a seasoning of pepper. Shape into two large flat burgers.

3   Heat a non-stick frying pan and dry-fry the burgers for 4–5 minutes on each side over a medium heat.

4   While the burgers are cooking, toast the rye bread until crisp. Mix the yogurt and horseradish sauce together with a seasoning of pepper. Spread the sauce on to each slice of toasted bread then place a salmon burger on top.

Try this

For pan-Asian tuna burgers: replace the salmon fillet with the same amount of fresh tuna. Add the egg white and breadcrumbs as above, but flavour with ½ teaspoon grated lime zest, 1 cm (½ inch) grated fresh root ginger, 2 tablespoons chopped fresh coriander and ¼ diced red chilli. Replace the horseradish-yogurt sauce with a sweet chilli mayo, made by combining 2 tablespoons light mayonnaise with 1 tablespoon Thai sweet chilli sauce, plus a squeeze of lime juice.

This hearty Middle Eastern-inspired chicken and pasta bake only needs a good serving of green beans to make it a complete meal.

Fragrant chicken and tomato pasta bake

Calories per serving 373

10 minutes preparation

35 minutes cooking

Serves 4

8 x 66 g (2¼ oz) small skinless boneless
    chicken thighs

1 red onion, sliced thickly

400 g can chopped tomatoes

600 ml (20 fl oz) chicken stock

juice of a small orange and zest of
    ½ the orange

½ teaspoon ground cinnamon

½ teaspoon ground cumin

175 g (6 oz) dried mini pasta shells

1   Preheat the oven to Gas Mark 6/200°C/fan oven 180°C.

2   Heat a non-stick frying pan over a high heat, add the chicken thighs, seam-side down, and brown for 3 minutes on each side, scattering the onion around the chicken to cook at the same time (there is no need for cooking spray).

3   Transfer the chicken and onion to a baking dish. Set aside. Add the tomatoes, stock, orange juice and zest to the frying pan then add the spices and pasta. Bring to the boil and pour over the chicken in the baking dish.

4   Cover the dish with foil, tucking it around the sides. Bake in the oven for 20 minutes then remove the foil and cook for a further 15 minutes until the pasta is tender and beginning to crisp up on top.

5   Leave to rest for 5 minutes before serving.

Try this

V Replace the chicken with 8 Quorn fillets and use vegetable stock instead.

For a lower fat option, use 600 g (1 lb 5 oz) chicken breasts instead of thighs.

Knock up a quick stir-fry for supper and serve with sugar snap peas.

Gingered pork noodles

Calories per serving 454
15 minutes in total
Serves 1

50 g (1¾ oz) dried egg noodles
calorie controlled cooking spray
1 small onion, sliced
100 g (3½ oz) pork fillet, trimmed of all visible fat
    and cut into strips
juice of a small orange
2 tablespoons Thai sweet chilli sauce
1 cm (½ inch) fresh root ginger, grated
1 tablespoon soy sauce
2 tablespoons shredded fresh basil

1   Bring a saucepan of water to the boil, add the noodles and return to the boil. Cook according to the packet instructions and then drain.
2   Meanwhile, heat a non-stick frying pan and spray with the cooking spray. Add the onion and pork and stir-fry for 4 minutes over a high heat until starting to brown.
3   Mix together the orange juice, chilli sauce, ginger and soy sauce. Add this mixture, plus the drained noodles, to the frying pan and cook for 1 minute, stirring to coat and mix together.
4   Add the basil, mix in quickly and serve immediately.

With everything cooked together in one dish, a traybake is such an easy way to get dinner on the table.

Easy chicken traybake

Calories per serving 395
10 minutes preparation
30 minutes cooking
Serves 4

600 g (1 lb 5 oz) sweet potatoes,
    peeled and chopped roughly
2 red peppers, de-seeded and chopped roughly
2 yellow peppers, de-seeded and chopped roughly
calorie controlled cooking spray
2 tablespoons wholegrain mustard
1 heaped teaspoon clear honey
2 tablespoons soy sauce
4 x 150 g (5½ oz) skinless boneless chicken breasts

1   Preheat the oven to Gas Mark 7/220°C/fan oven 200°C. Spread out the sweet potatoes and peppers on a large roasting tray and spray lightly with the cooking spray. Roast in the oven for 15 minutes.
2   Meanwhile, mix together the mustard, honey and soy sauce in a mixing bowl. Cut shallow slashes in each chicken breast, add to the bowl and turn to coat. When the initial cooking time is up, stir the vegetables around on the tray, place the chicken breasts on top and drizzle with the mustard sauce. Roast for a further 15 minutes or until the chicken is cooked through.

A mixed leaf salad, dressed with a touch of lemon juice, makes a delicious accompaniment for the burgers.

One of the quickest and easiest recipes in the book, this is a great choice when you've only got a few minutes to spare.

Lamb burgers with tzatziki

Calories per serving 366
10 minutes preparation
10 minutes cooking
❋ for uncooked burgers only
Serves 4

50 g (1¾ oz) fresh breadcrumbs
4 tablespoons skimmed milk
2 shallots, chopped finely
1¼ teaspoons dried mint
500 g (1 lb 2 oz) lean lamb mince
100 g (3½ oz) 0% fat Greek yogurt
75 g (2¾ oz) cucumber, diced
4 soft rolls, split
3 tomatoes, sliced

1 Preheat the grill. Mix the breadcrumbs, milk and shallots together in a mixing bowl with 1 teaspoon of the dried mint and the lamb mince. Shape into four large flat burgers.

2 Grill the lamb burgers for 5 minutes on each side, or until cooked to your liking.

3 Meanwhile, make the tzatziki. Mix together the yogurt with the remaining dried mint then stir in the cucumber.

4 Split each roll in half and lightly toast the cut sides of the rolls under the grill. Top with a few slices of tomato. Add a burger to each one then top with a spoonful of tzatziki and serve straightaway.

Spicy sticky turkey bites

Calories per serving 198
10 minutes in total
Serves 2

1 garlic clove, crushed
1 cm (½ inch) fresh root ginger, grated
1 tablespoon soy sauce
2 tablespoons tomato ketchup
1 tablespoon Thai sweet chilli sauce
1 teaspoon sesame oil
250 g (9 oz) skinless turkey breast, diced

1 Mix the garlic, ginger, soy sauce, ketchup, chilli sauce and sesame oil together and then stir in the turkey.

2 Heat a non-stick frying pan then add the turkey and marinate. Stir-fry for 5 minutes over a medium heat, stirring to make sure that the marinade doesn't stick and burn.

3 Add 100 ml (3½ fl oz) water to the frying pan and allow to bubble for 1 minute to make a sauce. Serve immediately.

Try this
If you're a mushroom fan, add 150 g (5½ oz) button mushrooms with the turkey.

Serve these lusciously light meatballs with 60 g (2 oz) dried rice, cooked according to the packet instructions, per person.

Curried Nordic meatballs

Calories per serving 240
20 minutes preparation
35 minutes cooking
Serves 6

500 g (1 lb 2 oz) extra lean pork mince
2 small onions, chopped finely
60 g (2 oz) plain flour
1½ tablespoons medium curry powder
100 ml (3½ fl oz) skimmed milk
1 egg
1 egg white
2 chicken stock cubes
2 carrots, peeled and sliced into
    thin half moons
1 leek, sliced
40 g (1½ oz) low fat spread
1 tablespoon half fat crème fraîche
1 apple, cored and sliced

1   In a food processor or bowl, combine the pork, half of the onion, 1 tablespoon flour, half a tablespoon of curry powder, the milk, egg and egg white. Mix together until thoroughly combined.

2   Bring a large saucepan of water to the boil and add one stock cube to the pan. Make the second stock cube up to 600 ml (20 fl oz) and reserve this for the sauce in step 4. Add the carrots and leek to the pan of stock. Simmer for 3 minutes then lift the vegetables out with a draining spoon. Reserve for later.

3   Using a tablespoon measure, scoop and shape the mince mixture into 30 meatballs. Dip the measure into a bowl of cold water before shaping each one so that the mixture doesn't stick to the spoon, then place the meatballs on a wet plate. Slide the meatballs into the pan of hot stock, a few at a time so that they don't all stick together before they are cooked. Bring the pan back to boiling point then simmer gently for 10 minutes.

4   While the meatballs are cooking melt the low fat spread in a lidded non stick saucepan. Add the rest of the onion plus 4 tablespoons of the stock reserved for the sauce, cover and cook for 3 minutes. Stir in the rest of the curry power and flour and cook for 1 minute then gradually add the rest of the stock, stirring all the time. Simmer for 10 minutes.

5   Drain the meatballs, return to the pan and add the curry sauce along with the crème fraîche, carrots, leeks and apples. Cook for 2–3 minutes until everything is heated through, then serve.

Shaping the mince mixture into little balls is so easy. Then simply drop them into boiling stock and they're ready in 10 minutes.

This colourful lasagne is terrific served with a crunchy salad of shredded Iceberg lettuce, coarsely grated carrot and cherry tomatoes.

Mexican bean lasagne

Calories per serving 393

20 minutes in total

45 minutes cooking

V ❋ Serves 6

calorie controlled cooking spray

1 pack of 3 mixed peppers, de-seeded
    and diced

1 red chilli, de-seeded and diced

2 teaspoons ground cumin

1 kg carton passata

1 x Simple White Sauce recipe
    (see page 20)

410 g can kidney beans in water,
    drained and rinsed

410 g can black eyed beans in water,
    drained and rinsed

326 g can sweetcorn, drained

4 tablespoons chopped fresh coriander

9 sheets dried no cook lasagne

50 g (1¾ oz) half fat mature cheese

1 Preheat the oven to Gas Mark 4/180°C/fan oven 160°C.

2 Heat a large lidded saucepan and spray with the cooking spray. Add the peppers and cook for 4–5 minutes over a high heat until starting to colour at the edges. Add the chilli and cumin and cook for a few seconds, stirring, to bring out the flavour, then add the passata. Bring to the boil and simmer, partially covered, for 10 minutes.

3 Meanwhile, make the Simple White Sauce, following the recipe on page 20.

4 Mix the beans, sweetcorn and coriander together. Spoon a third of the tomato and pepper sauce into the base of a rectangular baking dish, measuring 23 x 30 cm (9 x 12 inches) and then add three lasagne sheets. Top with half of the bean mixture then add further layers of tomato and pepper sauce, lasagne sheets, beans, tomato sauce and lasagne sheets. Finally, pour the white sauce evenly over the top and scatter over the cheese.

5 Bake in the oven for 35 minutes or until the pasta is tender and the top is bubbling. Cover with a sheet of foil if the top is browning too much.

6 Leave the lasagne to settle for 5–10 minutes once it is cooked, before slicing into portions (this makes it easier to serve without it falling apart).

Cheat's tip

Cut down on preparation time by replacing the fresh mixed peppers with 350 g (12 oz) frozen sliced peppers in step 1.

This recipe makes enough for four people to enjoy on one day and then you can freeze the rest to make another meal later such as the Lovely Lasagne (see page 132).

Brilliant Bolognese

Calories per serving 138

20 minutes preparation

30 minutes cooking

❋ Serves 8

2 onions, chopped roughly

2 carrots, peeled and chopped roughly

1 celery stick, chopped roughly

calorie controlled cooking spray

500 g pack extra lean beef mince

2 garlic cloves, crushed

125 ml (4 fl oz) red wine

2 x 400 g cans chopped tomatoes

1 teaspoon dried mixed herbs

300 ml (10 fl oz) beef stock

1   Place the onions, carrots and celery in a food processor and whizz until finely chopped, or chop finely by hand if you don't have a processor.

2   Heat a lidded flameproof casserole dish, spray lightly with the cooking spray, add the vegetable mixture and cook, covered, for 10 minutes until softened. Add a splash of water if the vegetables are starting to stick.

3   Meanwhile, heat a non stick frying pan and spray with the cooking spray. Add the mince, breaking up any lumps with a wooden spoon, and brown. You may need to do this in two batches unless you have a very large frying pan, as adding too much at once will mean that it is likely to boil in its own juices rather than fry and brown.

4   Remove the lid from the casserole, stir in the garlic and cook for 1 minute more. Now add the browned mince, the red wine, chopped tomatoes, herbs and beef stock. Bring to a simmer, partially cover the casserole and simmer for 30 minutes.

Try this

Ⅴ Replace the beef with the same quantity of Quorn mince. There's no need to brown it first, just add in step 4. Use vegetable stock instead of beef stock.

Instead of using red wine, increase the amount of stock to 425 ml (15 fl oz).

For Chilli Con Carne: leave out the red wine, but add 1 red and 1 green pepper, diced, and spice up the mince mixture with 2 teaspoons ground cumin, ½ teaspoon dried chilli flakes and 1 teaspoon cocoa powder, all added in step 4. After 15 minutes, stir in a 400 g can of kidney beans, rinsed and drained.

For Smoky Barbecue Beef Mince: omit the red wine and mixed herbs. Add 200 g (7 oz) chopped mushrooms and 1 teaspoon smoked paprika with the garlic in step 4. When you add the tomatoes, add 4 tablespoons barbecue sauce and 1 teaspoon soft dark brown sugar.

❋ **Freezer tip**

If freezing, make sure it is fully cool before freezing in a labelled container.

If you've already made the Brilliant Bolognese on page 131 and have some to use, it's a doddle to whip up a quick lasagne.

Lovely lasagne

Calories per serving 427

15 minutes preparation + 50 minutes
    making Brilliant Bolognese, if required

40 minutes cooking

✳ Serves 4

40 g (1½ oz) low fat spread

40 g (1½ oz) plain flour

450 ml (16 fl oz) skimmed milk

1 bay leaf

½ x Brilliant Bolognese recipe
    (see page 131) or see Cheat's tip

6 sheets no precook dried lasagne

125 g pack reduced fat mozzarella
    cheese, diced

15 g (½ oz) freshly grated Parmesan
    cheese

1 If you don't already have some in the fridge or freezer to use, make a full quantity of Brilliant Bolognese following the recipe on page 131. Use half for this lasagne and then, once cool, freeze the remainder to use another time.

2 Preheat the oven to Gas Mark 4/180°C/fan oven 160°C. To make a white sauce, place the low fat spread, flour, skimmed milk and bay leaf in a non stick saucepan. Cook over a medium-high heat, stirring all the time to avoid lumps, until the sauce comes to the boil. Simmer for 2 minutes then remove the bay leaf.

3 Spread a quarter of the white sauce over the base of an 18 cm (7 inch) square baking dish. Add a third each of the Bolognese and the mozzarella and top with two sheets of lasagne.

4 Repeat to make two more sets of layers of Bolognese, mozzarella and lasagne. Pour the rest of the white sauce evenly over the lasagne and scatter the Parmesan cheese on top.

5 Bake in the centre of the oven for 40 minutes or until the pasta is tender and the top of the lasagne is golden brown and crisp at the edges.

Cheat's tip

Brown 250 g (9 oz) extra lean beef mince then add 200 g (7 oz) chopped mushrooms and a 500 g jar of light bolognese sauce. Simmer for 10 minutes before using in the lasagne.

Layer up the sheets of lasagne with Bolognese sauce, white sauce and mozzarella for a great mid-week meal.

If you want to treat yourself and a loved one, this special recipe is ideal. Serve with mange tout along with mashed carrot and swede.

Wine-glazed duck breasts with figs

Calories per serving 258

20 minutes in total

Serves 2

calorie controlled cooking spray

2 x 125 g (4½ oz) skinless boneless
    duck breasts

4 fresh figs, halved

1 shallot, sliced thinly

1 tablespoon balsamic vinegar

1 heaped teaspoon clear honey

125 ml (4 fl oz) red wine

150 ml (5 fl oz) chicken stock

½ a cinnamon stick

1   Heat a non stick frying pan over a medium heat and spray lightly with the cooking spray. Add the duck breasts and cook for 5 minutes. Turn the duck and cook for 2 minutes then add the figs, cut side down, plus the sliced shallot. Cook for 3 minutes then remove the duck breasts to a plate and keep warm.

2   Add the balsamic vinegar and honey to the frying pan and turn the figs over in the mixture for 30 seconds before transferring them to the plate with the duck.

3   Pour the red wine and stock into the frying pan, add the cinnamon stick and boil the sauce for 5 minutes over a high heat until reduced and syrupy. Briefly return the duck and figs to the pan and turn to glaze in the sticky sauce. Serve on warmed plates.

Cook's tip
Although duck has a lot of fat when cooked with the skin on, skinless duck breasts are a great lean option and an excellent choice to add a little variety to your meals.

Try this
Replace the duck breasts with 2 x 150 g (5½ oz) skinless boneless chicken breasts, if you prefer.

CHAPTER : 6

Make it
simple

The zingy, fresh flavours of this hearty main meal salad go so well with the warm halloumi cheese which is pan-fried to give it a soft texture and a tasty golden crust.

Halloumi with warm lemony bean salad

Calories per serving 331
20 minutes in total
V Serves 2

calorie controlled cooking spray
1 courgette, diced
1 shallot, chopped roughly
½ red chilli, de-seeded and diced
2 ripe tomatoes, chopped roughly
410 g can cannellini beans in water,
  drained and rinsed
100 g (3½ oz) halloumi, sliced
1 tablespoon lemon juice plus
  ½ teaspoon grated zest
1 teaspoon extra virgin olive oil
1 tablespoon chopped fresh mint
freshly ground black pepper

1 Spray a saucepan with the cooking spray, add the courgette, shallot and chilli and stir-fry for 3–4 minutes until starting to colour. Add the tomatoes and cannellini beans and heat for 2 minutes.

2 Meanwhile, heat a non stick frying pan and spray with the cooking spray. Season the halloumi with pepper then fry over a medium heat for 2 minutes on each side until golden brown.

3 Add the lemon juice and zest, olive oil and mint to the warm bean salad and divide between two plates. Place the halloumi on top and serve immediately.

Cheat's tip
Replace the lemon juice and olive oil with 1 tablespoon of low fat salad dressing.

Try this
You can replace the cannellini beans with a variety of different beans. Butter beans are particularly good in this recipe.

Add 1 roasted red pepper, de-seeded, peeled and cut into strips (see page 64) to add another delicious texture.

This delicious supper dish is something special, yet it is very quick to make. Using raw prawns rather then ready-cooked ones makes it taste more succulently juicy.

Tiger prawn tagliatelle

Calories per serving 329
15 minutes in total
Serves 2

225 g (8 oz) raw peeled tiger prawns
125 g (4½ oz) dried tagliatelle
calorie controlled cooking spray
300 g (10½ oz) ripe tomatoes,
    chopped roughly
½ red chilli, de-seeded and sliced
40 g (1½ oz) wild rocket
½ teaspoon grated lemon zest
freshly ground black pepper

1 Start by de-veining the prawns. Use a small sharp knife to make a shallow incision down the back of each prawn, exposing the intestinal tract. Use the tip of the knife to lift out this vein – it won't be visible in all cases, only if there are brown/black spots along the length of it. Set the prepared prawns aside.

2 Bring a saucepan of water to the boil, add the tagliatelle and cook for 10 minutes, or according to the packet instructions, until tender.

3 Meanwhile, heat a medium lidded saucepan and spray lightly with the cooking spray. Add the tomatoes, chilli and seasoning then cook over a medium-high heat for 3–4 minutes until the tomatoes start to break up.

4 Add the prawns and 4 tablespoons of the pasta cooking water to the pan with the tomatoes. The prawns will start to turn from grey to pink as soon as they come into contact with the heat. Cover the pan and cook gently for 3 minutes, stirring once or twice, until the prawns are cooked and pink throughout. Take care not to overcook the prawns or they will be dry, tough and rubbery.

5 Drain the tagliatelle and return to the pan. Add the prawns in the tomato sauce then add the rocket and lemon zest. Toss everything to mix together and then serve in warmed bowls.

This speedy supper dish can be on the table in just 10 minutes. It's lovely with 150 g (5½ oz) boiled new potatoes and some broccoli florets.

Pan-fried tuna with warm tomato and caper dressing

Calories per serving 273

10 minutes in total

Serves 1

1 tablespoon capers in brine

15 g (½ oz) pitted black olives in brine, chopped roughly

calorie controlled cooking spray

125 g (4½ oz) fresh tuna steak

2 tomatoes, chopped roughly

1 heaped tablespoon chopped fresh basil

1 teaspoon extra virgin olive oil

½ teaspoon grated lemon zest plus 1 teaspoon lemon juice

25 g (1 oz) wild rocket

freshly ground black pepper

1 Place the capers and olives in a small bowl, cover with water and leave to soak for a few minutes, to draw out some of the saltiness of the brine they are preserved in.

2 Heat a non stick frying pan and spray lightly with the cooking spray.

3 Season the tuna with black pepper then add to the hot pan and cook for 2–3 minutes on each side, depending on the thickness of your tuna steak.

4 Meanwhile, mix the tomatoes, basil, olive oil, lemon zest and juice together in a bowl. Drain the capers and olives and stir into the mixture, adding 1 tablespoon of cold water.

5 Tip this dressing into the frying pan around the tuna and cook for 30 seconds to just heat through whilst still maintaining its fresh flavour.

6 Serve the tuna steak on the rocket, with the dressing spooned over the top.

Try this

The warm tomato and caper dressing works well with a variety of meats: try a 150 g (5½ oz) skinless boneless chicken breast (10–12 minutes to cook), a 125 g (4½ oz) turkey breast steak (6 minutes to cook) or a 100 g (3½ oz) lean pork loin steak (8 minutes to cook).

These juicy pork steaks with plums are wonderful served with mashed potato. Allow 200 g (7 oz) boiled potatoes mashed with 1 tablespoon skimmed milk per person. Lightly cooked green cabbage goes very well on the side.

Pork steaks with plums, ginger and soy

Calories per serving 252

20 minutes in total

Serves 4

calorie controlled cooking spray

4 x 125 g (4½ oz) lean pork loin steaks

150 ml (5 fl oz) chicken stock

3 heaped teaspoons damson or
    plum jam

½ teaspoon ground ginger

1 garlic clove, crushed

1 teaspoon lemon juice

1 tablespoon soy sauce

½ teaspoon Dijon mustard

4 plums, stoned and quartered

1   Heat a large, lidded, non stick frying pan and spray with the cooking spray. Brown the pork steaks for 2 minutes on each side over a high heat.

2   Meanwhile, mix together the stock, jam, ginger, garlic, lemon juice, soy sauce and mustard to make a sauce.

3   Pour the sauce over the pork steaks, cover the pan and simmer for 5 minutes.

4   Scatter the plums amongst the pork steaks and simmer for 5 minutes more until the plums are starting to soften. Serve immediately.

Try this

You can also make this recipe with 4 x 125 g (4½ oz) skinless boneless chicken breasts.

This dish is so tasty with little cubes of oven-roasted potato – allow 150 g (5½ oz) cubed unpeeled potato, sprayed with a little calorie controlled cooking spray, per serving. Use a large roasting tin and cook the potatoes for 15 minutes on their own then add the vegetables and stuffed chicken to the tin so they can all cook together.

Chicken breasts stuffed with green olives and goat's cheese

Calories per serving 324

10 minutes preparation

20 minutes cooking

Serves 2

1 red onion, chopped roughly

175 g (6 oz) cherry tomatoes, halved

1 heaped teaspoon chopped fresh thyme

calorie controlled cooking spray

50 g (1¾ oz) soft goat's cheese

25 g (1 oz) pitted green olives, chopped

2 x 150 g (5½ oz) skinless boneless
     chicken breasts

1 Preheat the oven to Gas Mark 6/200°C/fan oven 180°C. Toss the onion, tomatoes and most of the thyme together on a non stick baking tray. Spray lightly with the cooking spray. Spread out into an even layer, making space in the centre of the tray.

2 Mix the goat's cheese and olives together with the rest of the thyme.

3 Use a sharp knife to cut a horizontal pocket into each chicken breast. Try to keep the opening quite narrow, but use the tip of the knife to open up a deeper pocket within the chicken breast. Be careful not to cut all the way through to the other side.

4 Use a teaspoon to stuff the goat's cheese mixture into each chicken breast. Press the chicken breast lightly closed around the stuffing.

5 Nestle the chicken amongst the vegetables on the baking tray and spray lightly with the cooking spray. Roast in the oven for 20 minutes, or until the chicken is cooked through, stirring the vegetables around halfway through.

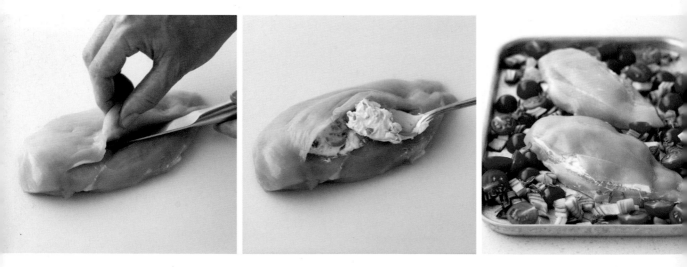

This speedy main meal is quick to make and great fun to eat but don't forget the napkin. Serve with a leafy green salad on the side.

Caramelised pepper and houmous wraps

Calories per serving 207

15 minutes in total

V Serves 2

2 medium flour tortillas

calorie controlled cooking spray

1 red or yellow pepper, de-seeded
   and sliced

1 courgette, cut into sticks

¼ teaspoon ground cumin

a pinch of chilli powder

1 tomato, chopped roughly

1 tablespoon reduced fat houmous

2 tablespoons 0% fat Greek yogurt

1   Heat a non stick frying pan. Warm each tortilla in the dry pan for 10 seconds each side to make it more flexible, then set aside.

2   Spray the pan with the cooking spray and stir-fry the pepper and courgette for 3 minutes over a high heat until starting to caramelise at the edges. Add the cumin, chilli and tomato and cook for 1 minute.

3   Meanwhile, mix the houmous and Greek yogurt together and spread on to the tortillas. Pile on the caramelised vegetables, roll up and cut in half to serve.

Cheat's tip

Replace the pepper and courgette with 175 g (6 oz) frozen roasted vegetables, to cut down on preparation time.

Try this

For prawn fajitas: replace the courgette with a sliced onion and add 100 g (3½ oz) cooked, peeled king prawns with the spices and tomato. Leave out the houmous and increase the 0% fat Greek yogurt to 3 tablespoons. Add a sprinkling of freshly chopped coriander to serve, if you wish.

The classic combination of steak and mushrooms works together beautifully in this recipe's creamy sauce. Toss together a mixed leaf salad and add some finely sliced mange tout for some crunch.

Steak and mushroom tagliatelle

Calories per serving 443
20 minutes in total
Serves 2

100 g (3½ oz) dried tagliatelle
225 g (8 oz) sirloin steak, trimmed of
    all visible fat
250 g (9 oz) mushrooms, sliced
100 ml (3½ fl oz) beef stock
1 garlic clove, crushed
1 tablespoon chopped fresh tarragon or
    1 teaspoon dried
100 g (3½ oz) low fat soft cheese
freshly ground black pepper

1   Bring a pan of water to the boil, add the pasta and then cook for 10 minutes or according to the packet instructions.

2   Meanwhile, heat a non stick frying pan and season the steak with pepper. Dry-fry the steak for 3–4 minutes on each side, depending on the thickness of the steak. Transfer to a plate and leave to rest for a few minutes before slicing thinly.

3   While the steak and tagliatelle are cooking, place the mushrooms in a lidded saucepan with the stock, garlic and tarragon. Cover and cook for 7–8 minutes or until softened. Stir in the soft cheese to make a creamy sauce.

4   Drain the tagliatelle and toss with the sliced steak and the mushroom sauce. Serve in warmed bowls.

Try this

V *For mushroom tagliatelle:* leave out the steak altogether and increase the mushrooms to 400 g (14 oz). Use a mixture of mushrooms, such as flat mushrooms or chestnut mushrooms, and replace the beef stock with vegetable stock.

For chicken and mushroom tagliatelle: use 250 g (9 oz) skinless chicken breasts in place of the sirloin steak. These will take longer to pan-fry; allow about 6 minutes on each side and check that they are cooked through by piercing the middle with a sharp knife. There should be no trace of pink.

Cheat's tip
Use a pack of ready-sliced mushrooms to speed up the preparation time.

What an inspired combination of flavours – all this recipe needs are some fine green beans on the side.

Seared salmon on warm Puy lentil salad

Calories per serving 440

30 minutes in total

Serves 4

150 g (5½ oz) dried puy lentils, rinsed

600 ml (20 fl oz) vegetable stock

1 onion, chopped finely

1 carrot, peeled and diced

1 celery stick, diced

4 x 125 g (4½ oz) salmon fillets

40 g (1½ oz) dried cranberries

2 teaspoons walnut oil

1 tablespoon balsamic vinegar

2 tablespoons chopped fresh parsley

1   Put the lentils in a lidded saucepan with 500 ml (18 fl oz) of the stock, bring to the boil. Cover and cook for 25 minutes or until tender.

2   Meanwhile, place the onion, carrot and celery in another lidded pan with the rest of the stock. Cover and cook for 10 minutes. Remove the lid and cook for 4–5 minutes, stirring occasionally, until softened.

3   Heat a non stick frying pan over a medium heat and add the salmon fillets. Cook for 3–4 minutes on each side (cooking spray is not necessary).

4   Drain the lentils and mix with the vegetables, cranberries, walnut oil, balsamic vinegar and parsley.

5   Serve the salmon on a bed of the warm puy lentil salad.

Cheat's tip

Cut down on cooking time by replacing the dried lentils with 2 x 400 g cans cooked puy lentils in water. Heat the lentils in the liquid from the can for 2–3 minutes, then drain and mix with the other ingredients for the warm salad, as in step 4.

Try this

The warm lentil salad is also delicious served with plain grilled chicken; allow 150 g (5½ oz) skinless boneless chicken breast per person.

A simple but satisfying twist on sausages and mash. Serve with baby Chantenay carrots to complete your meal.

Sausages with crushed new potatoes

Calories per serving 373

10 minutes preparation

20 minutes cooking

Serves 4

600 g (1 lb 5 oz) new potatoes

8 reduced fat sausages

calorie controlled cooking spray

1 bunch spring onions, sliced

250 g (9 oz) frozen peas

125 ml (4 fl oz) vegetable stock

100 g (3½ oz) Weight Watchers low fat
    soft cheese with Roasted Onion
    and Chives (see Cook's tip)

2 tablespoons chopped fresh mint

grated zest and juice of ½ a small lemon

1   Bring a lidded saucepan of water to the boil, add the new potatoes and return to the boil. Cover and cook for 15–20 minutes or until tender (the exact timing will depend on the size of the potatoes). Preheat the grill to medium.

2   Meanwhile, line the grill pan with foil and grill the sausages for 15–20 minutes, turning once or twice so they brown evenly.

3   Spray a saucepan with the cooking spray and stir-fry the spring onions for 1 minute. Add the peas and stock and cook for 4 minutes. Mix in the soft cheese and half of the mint to make a creamy sauce.

4   Drain the new potatoes and crush roughly using a potato masher. Add the lemon zest and juice plus the remaining mint.

5   Divide the crushed potatoes between four warmed plates and top each with two sausages. Spoon the creamy pea sauce over the sausages and potatoes and serve straightaway.

Cook's tip

If you can't find the Weight Watchers branded flavoured low fat soft cheese, replace with plain low fat soft cheese and add 1 garlic clove, crushed, as additional flavouring.

V Try this

Use Quorn sausages in place of the pork sausages, cooked according to the packet instructions.

Keeping a meaty theme, use 8 Weight Watchers Premium Pork Sausages.

This speedy recipe can be ready in only 15 minutes plus there's no need for any side dishes since everything you need is already included.

Oregano lamb steaks with chopped summer salad

Calories per serving 224

15 minutes in total

Serves 2

100 g (3½ oz) dried giant couscous
   (see Cook's tip)

2 tablespoons chopped fresh mint

½ teaspoon dried oregano

a pinch of smoked paprika

grated zest and juice of ½ a small lemon

2 x 100 g (3½ oz) boneless lean lamb
   leg steaks

75 g (2¾ oz) Iceberg lettuce, chopped

75 g (2¾ oz) cucumber, diced

3 tomatoes, chopped roughly

1   Bring a saucepan of water to the boil, add the couscous and return to the boil. Cook for 8 minutes until tender, or according to the packet instructions. Drain and mix with half the chopped mint.

2   Meanwhile, mix the oregano and smoked paprika with the lemon zest and half of the juice to make a spice paste. Rub this into the lamb steaks.

3   Heat a non stick frying pan, add the lamb steaks and fry for 3–4 minutes on each side over a medium heat, until cooked to your liking.

4   Meanwhile, mix the chopped lettuce, cucumber and tomatoes together with the rest of the lemon juice and mint.

5   Serve the lamb steaks with the minted giant couscous and the chopped summer salad.

Cook's tips

Giant couscous is, as the name implies, a larger version of the more traditional small-grained couscous. It has a texture similar to pasta, and is cooked by simmering in boiling water or stock. If you prefer to use regular couscous, use the same dried weight of couscous but prepare it in the following manner: place in a bowl, add 175 ml (6 fl oz) boiling water or vegetable stock and give it a good stir. Cover the bowl with a plate or with cling film and leave to stand for 5 minutes to absorb the liquid and to soften. Mix in 1 tablespoon of chopped fresh mint before serving.

These tasty lamb steaks can also be cooked on a preheated barbecue over a medium heat for 3–4 minutes on each side, or until cooked to your liking.

Try this

Try replacing the lamb steaks with 2 x 125 g (4½ oz) turkey breast steaks.

V Replace the lamb with 100 g (3½ oz) halloumi, sliced, per person. The halloumi will only need 2 minutes on each side on a medium heat.

A complete meal in a parcel, this fish dish is particularly colourful if you use golden yellow smoked haddock rather than the natural undyed type.

Smoked haddock and potato parcels

Calories per serving 267

20 minutes preparation

15 minutes cooking

Serves 2

250 g (9 oz) new potatoes, sliced
3–4 mm thick

2 x 150 g (5½ oz) smoked haddock fillets

a squeeze of lemon juice plus
½ teaspoon grated lemon zest

100 g (3½ oz) cherry tomatoes, halved

75 g (2¾ oz) frozen peas

75 g (2¾ oz) asparagus tips

1 tablespoon chopped fresh basil

1 tablespoon chopped fresh parsley

freshly ground black pepper

1 Preheat the oven to Gas Mark 4/180°C/fan oven 160°C. Bring a saucepan of water to the boil, add the potato slices and return to the boil. Cook for 5–7 minutes until tender then drain.

2 Meanwhile, cut two large rectangles of baking parchment, each approximately 35 x 50 cm (14 x 20 inches). Fold each one in half to make a seam then open it out again. Working on one half of each piece of parchment, place the potatoes in the centre. Position the smoked haddock on top. Season with pepper, adding a squeeze of lemon juice.

3 Mix the tomatoes, peas, asparagus and herbs together then tumble the mixture over the fish. Add 1 tablespoon of water to each parcel then fold the parchment back over the top of the ingredients.

4 The next step is to seal the parcels. Working from the end of one edge, fold one corner up to make a narrow triangle about 5 cm (2 inches) long. Make another fold in the same way, starting halfway along the first triangle so the point is sealed in as you fold, and repeat all the way around the parcel – this is much easier to do than it may sound. You will end up with something that looks rather like a large Cornish pasty. Alternatively, you can simply fold the edges over a couple of times and secure in a few places with paper clips. Just remember that the clips will be hot when you take the parcels out of the oven so take care with them.

5 Place the parcels on a large baking tray and bake in the oven for 15 minutes, by which time the fish should be cooked through and starting to flake, but still lovely and moist.

6 Open the parcels carefully and then serve immediately.

Sealing the smoked haddock and veggies together in a paper parcel creates a lovely, fragrant dish.

Couscous is an excellent accompaniment to this dish, and can easily be prepared while the main dish is being cooked. Place 100 g (3½ oz) dried weight of couscous in a bowl and stir in 175 ml (6 fl oz) boiling water. Cover and leave to stand and soften for 5 minutes before fluffing up with a fork. Stir in some chopped fresh coriander to complement the pork, if you wish.

Zesty coriander pork with stir-fried kale

Calories per serving 244

20 minutes in total

Serves 2

grated zest of ½ a lemon

2 heaped tablespoons chopped fresh
    coriander

250 g (9 oz) lean pork fillet, cut into
    1 cm (½ inch) slices

calorie controlled cooking spray

½ red chilli, de-seeded and sliced

1 garlic clove, crushed

2.5 cm (1 inch) fresh root ginger, grated

175 g (6 oz) kale, washed, de-stalked
    and chopped

1 Mix the lemon zest and coriander together on a plate and press the slices of pork fillet into the mixture to coat. Heat a large non stick frying pan and lightly spray with the cooking spray.

2 Fry the pork for 2 minutes on each side or until cooked through then transfer to a plate and keep warm.

3 Add the chilli, garlic and ginger to the frying pan and stir-fry for 1 minute. Add the kale and stir-fry for 4–5 minutes until tender. The kale will collapse as it cooks, in much the same way as spinach, so don't be alarmed by the large amount when you first put it in the pan.

4 Serve the kale with the zesty coriander pork.

Try this

Substitute 2 x 125 g (4½ oz) turkey steaks for the pork fillet and there's no need to slice the turkey.

It's also delicious with 2 x 100 g (3½ oz) fresh mackerel fillets in place of the sliced pork fillet. Cook the mackerel on each side for 3 minutes until the fish begins to flake easily.

This is based on a traditional pasta dish from the Italian region around Genoa, and is usually made with either wholemeal pasta, or with trofie pasta, which is a rolled 'quill' shape. Serve with a cherry tomato and red onion salad.

This quick and easy pasta dish has a fabulously rich, savoury flavour, and is an unusual way to use lean duck breast meat.

Pasta alla genovese

Calories per serving 336
5 minutes preparation
15 minutes cooking
V Serves 4

300 g (10½ oz) new potatoes, diced
200 g (7 oz) green beans, trimmed
200 g (7 oz) dried wholemeal pasta shells
60 g (2 oz) pesto
100 g (3½ oz) low fat soft cheese

1 Bring two saucepans of water to the boil. Add the new potatoes to one pan and cook for 10 minutes or until just tender. Add the green beans to the same pan and cook for a further 4 minutes until both potatoes and beans are cooked.

2 Meanwhile, add the pasta to the second pan of water and cook for 10 minutes until tender or according to the packet instructions.

3 Mix the pesto and soft cheese together in a bowl.

4 Drain the pasta, reserving half a mugful of the pasta cooking water. Drain the potatoes and beans then mix together in whichever pan is larger. Add the pesto mixture plus 4 tablespoons of the reserved pasta cooking water to give a creamy sauce of coating consistency.

5 Serve immediately in warmed bowls.

Duck and mushroom linguine

Calories per serving 303
15 minutes in total
Serves 2

75 g (2¾ oz) dried linguine
100 g (3½ oz) Savoy cabbage, shredded
calorie controlled cooking spray
150 g (5½ oz) skinless duck breast, cut into thin strips
3 bacon medallions, cut into thin strips
2 shallots, sliced thinly
150 g (5½ oz) mushrooms, sliced
1 garlic clove, crushed
125 ml (4 fl oz) chicken stock

1 Bring a large saucepan of water to the boil, add the linguine and bring back to the boil. Cook for 8 minutes, or until nearly tender, then add the cabbage and cook for a further 3 minutes.

2 Meanwhile, heat a non stick frying pan. Spray lightly with the cooking spray then add the duck, bacon and shallots. Stir-fry at a high heat for 3 minutes.

3 Add the mushrooms, garlic and stock and cook for another 3 minutes, stirring frequently.

4 Drain the linguine and cabbage then toss together with the duck and mushroom mixture. Serve immediately in warmed bowls.

A wonderful treat for when it's just you and you fancy a flavoursome juicy steak. It's very quick to make and tastes great with a grilled flat mushroom and some tenderstem broccoli on the side.

Glazed steak with marbled pea and potato mash

Calories per serving 410

20 minutes in total

Serves 1

1 tablespoon soy sauce

1 teaspoon sesame oil

125 g (4½ oz) lean beef fillet steak

150 g (5½ oz) potatoes,
    peeled and chopped roughly

75 g (2¾ oz) frozen peas

1 small garlic clove, crushed

1 tablespoon skimmed milk

freshly ground black pepper

1   Mix the soy sauce and sesame oil together with black pepper in a shallow dish. Turn the steak in the mixture to coat well and set aside for 5–10 minutes.

2   Bring a saucepan of water to the boil. Add the potatoes, return to the boil and cook for 12–15 minutes until tender.

3   Meanwhile, heat a non stick frying pan. Remove the steak from the marinade and dry-fry it for 2–3 minutes on each side over a medium heat. Remove the steak to a warmed plate and keep warm.

4   While the steak is cooking place the peas in a small lidded pan with the garlic and 3 tablespoons water. Cook for 5 minutes then tip the peas and their cooking juices into a tall jug or similar container. Use a hand blender to blend to a purée.

5   Drain the potatoes and mash with the milk. Gently stir in the pea purée to give a marbled appearance then serve with the steak.

Cook's tip

The timings in the recipe allow for a medium-rare steak, although it will also depend on thickness. If you prefer your steak well done then cook it for about 4 minutes on each side.

Try this

If you want this recipe to serve two people, double all of the ingredients except the soy sauce and sesame oil.

These parcels are a great make-ahead meal - especially if you have people eating at different times. They can simply be popped in the oven when you are ready to cook them. If you are cooking the parcels straight from chilled, be sure to allow an extra 5 minutes oven time to ensure that the chicken is cooked through.

Oriental chicken and noodles en papillote

Calories per serving 449

10 minutes preparation

20 minutes cooking

Serves 2

125 g (4½ oz) dried egg noodles

2 tablespoons soy sauce

½ red chilli, de-seeded and diced

1 cm (½ inch) fresh root ginger, grated

1 garlic clove, crushed

calorie controlled cooking spray

125 g (4½ oz) shiitake mushrooms, halved

200 g (7 oz) pak choi, quartered
   lengthways

50 g (1¾ oz) baby leaf spinach

2 x 125 g (4½ oz) skinless boneless
   chicken breasts

1   Bring a saucepan of water to the boil, add the noodles and return to the boil. Cook for 2 minutes or until just starting to soften. The noodles will finish cooking inside the parcels so don't cook them completely at this stage. Drain and set aside.

2   Mix together the soy sauce, chill, ginger, garlic and 1 tablespoon cold water. Set aside.

3   Preheat the oven to Gas Mark 4/180°C/fan oven 160°C. Cut two large rectangles of foil, each measuring approximately 35 x 70 cm (14 x 28 inches). Fold in half then open up again and spray lightly with the cooking spray. Working on one half of each piece of foil, place the noodles in the centre. Add the mushrooms, pak choi and spinach leaves then place a chicken breast on top and drizzle with the soy sauce mixture. Fold the other half of foil over the top of the ingredients then fold the edges over a couple of times to seal the parcel. Place on a baking tray.

4   Bake the parcels for 20 minutes, by which time the chicken should be cooked through, and the vegetables will be tender. Carefully tear the parcels open, bearing in mind that hot steam will be released. Transfer to warmed plates to serve.

Try this

If you want to ring the changes, replace the chicken breasts with 2 x 125 g (4½ oz) skinless salmon fillets. Leave out the shiitake mushrooms and replace with the same amount of asparagus tips. These parcels will only need to be cooked for 15 minutes.

Cheat's tip

Replace the shiitake mushrooms, pak choi and spinach with 200 g (7 oz) ready-prepared stir-fry vegetables.

An attractive and colourful salsa accompanies these quick-to-cook turkey steaks. Serve them with sugar snap peas and cook 60 g (2 oz) dried brown rice per person.

Turkey steaks with mango and avocado salsa

Calories per serving 240

15 minutes in total

Serves 4

1 lime

1 heaped teaspoon clear honey

4 x 125 g (4½ oz) turkey steaks

1 ripe avocado, diced

1 ripe mango, peeled, stoned and diced

½ red chilli, de-seeded and diced

½ small red onion, chopped finely

1 tablespoon chopped fresh coriander

calorie controlled cooking spray

freshly ground black pepper

1 Grate the zest from half of the lime and squeeze out all of the juice. Mix the zest and half of the lime juice with the honey in a shallow dish with a seasoning of pepper. Add the turkey steaks and turn to coat in the mixture. Set aside while you make the salsa.

2 In a mixing bowl, toss the avocado with the rest of the lime juice then mix with the mango, chilli, onion, coriander and black pepper to taste.

3 Heat a large non stick frying pan and spray lightly with the cooking spray. Remove the turkey steaks from their marinade, add to the pan and cook for 2½ minutes on each side until cooked through. Serve immediately, accompanied by the salsa.

Cook's tip

Preparing a mango is easy: simply use a swivel-headed vegetable peeler to remove the skin then slice the flesh away from the flat-centred stone.

Try this

The mango and avocado salsa also works beautifully with salmon. Replace the turkey steaks with 4 x 125 g (4½ oz) skinless salmon fillets. Pan-fry for 3–4 minutes on each side to cook through.

CHAPTER : 7

The modern vegetarian

These home-made gnocchi are very easy to prepare, and have a much lighter texture than ready-prepared ones. Serve with a rocket, watercress and spinach salad.

Ricotta gnocchi with cherry tomato and basil sauce

Calories per serving 457

20 minutes in total

V Serves 2

For the sauce

250 g (9 oz) cherry tomatoes, quartered

1 garlic clove, crushed

1 tablespoon chopped fresh basil

5 tablespoons vegetable stock

½ teaspoon caster sugar

For the gnocchi

125 g (4½ oz) ricotta cheese

125 g (4½ oz) low fat soft cheese

25 g (1 oz) freshly grated vegetarian hard
    Italian cheese

100 g (3½ oz) plain flour

salt and freshly ground black pepper

1 Place all the sauce ingredients in a lidded saucepan, bring to the boil and simmer, partially covered, for 8–10 minutes until slightly thickened. Bring a large saucepan of water to the boil, ready to cook the gnocchi.

2 To make the gnocchi, mix the ricotta, soft cheese, hard Italian cheese and seasoning together in a mixing bowl using a wooden spoon. Reserve 2 teaspoons of the flour for rolling out then mix the rest into the cheese mixture to make a soft but not sticky dough.

3 Divide the gnocchi dough into four balls. Dust the work surface lightly with the reserved flour and roll each ball out by hand into a long sausage shape, measuring about 2 cm (¾ inch) in diameter and 30 cm (12 inches) long.

4 Line up the gnocchi rolls then cut each into 2 cm (¾ inch) sections. Drop these into the pan of boiling water. Bring back to the boil and simmer for 2 minutes. As the gnocchi cook, they will rise to the surface.

5 Use a draining spoon to lift the gnocchi out of the pan (they are too soft and delicate to be drained in a colander) and divide between two warmed bowls. Spoon the sauce over the gnocchi to serve.

Cheat's tip

You can use 125 g (4½ oz) ready-made gnocchi per person, cooked according to the packet instructions, and served with this sauce.

Terrific served with a Naan Bread (see page 30).

Pea and sweet potato korma

Calories per serving 245

10 minutes preparation

25 minutes cooking

V Serves 2

1 onion, sliced

250 ml (9 fl oz) vegetable stock

2 teaspoons korma curry paste

1 garlic clove, crushed

1 cm (½ inch) fresh root ginger, grated

1 teaspoon ground cumin

200 g (7 oz) chopped tomatoes

250 g (9 oz) sweet potatoes, peeled and
    diced

100 g (3½ oz) green beans, trimmed and
    halved

75 g (2¾ oz) frozen peas

2 tablespoons virtually fat-free
    plain yogurt

1 Place the onion in a lidded saucepan with 4 tablespoons of the stock. Cover and cook over a medium heat for 8 minutes until softened. Add the korma paste, garlic, ginger and ground cumin and cook for 1 minute, stirring, to bring out the flavours.

2 Mix in the tomatoes and the rest of the stock and simmer, covered for 10 minutes.

3 Meanwhile, bring a saucepan of water to the boil. Add the sweet potatoes, bring back to the boil and cook for 3 minutes. Add the green beans to the pan and cook for 3 minutes more until both sweet potatoes and beans are just tender. Drain.

4 Mix the sweet potatoes, green beans and the frozen peas into the curry sauce. Cook for 3 minutes for the flavours to meld.

5 Serve the curry with the yogurt drizzled on top.

These little kofte are similar to falafel so you might like to try stuffing them into a medium pitta bread to enjoy.

Chick pea and courgette kofte with tabbouleh

Calories per serving 204

30 minutes in total

V ✳ for kofte only

Serves 4

For the tabbouleh

175 g (6 oz) dried bulgur wheat

4 tablespoons chopped fresh parsley

2 tablespoons chopped fresh chives

3 tablespoons chopped fresh mint

3 tomatoes, chopped roughly

100 g (3½ oz) cucumber, diced

grated zest and juice of ½ a lemon

For the kofte

calorie controlled cooking spray

1 red onion, grated

2 courgettes, grated

½ teaspoon smoked paprika

1 teaspoon ground cumin

410 g can chick peas in water, drained and rinsed

½ tablespoon plain flour

150 g (5½ oz) 0% fat Greek yogurt

1   To make the tabbouleh, place the bulgur wheat in a saucepan, add cold water to cover then bring to the boil and cook for 10 minutes until tender. Drain well and mix the bulgur wheat with the fresh herbs, tomatoes, cucumber, lemon juice and half the zest. Set aside until ready to serve.

2   Meanwhile, to make the kofte, heat a non stick frying pan and spray lightly with the cooking spray. Stir-fry the onion and courgette for 5 minutes over a high heat until the mixture has wilted and most of the moisture has evaporated. Add the spices and cook for 1 minute to bring out the flavour.

3   In a bowl, crush the chick peas using a potato masher. Add the rest of the lemon zest and the cooked vegetable mixture and mix together well. Shape into 12 patties then dust with flour.

4   Wipe out the frying pan with a piece of kitchen paper and spray with a little more cooking spray. Fry the kofte for 3 minutes on each side until golden brown and piping hot. Serve with the tabbouleh, accompanied by the Greek yogurt.

A lovely recipe that is perfect for a quick supper. Serve with a tomato and red onion salad.

Garlic mushroom and rustic bean bruschetta

Calories per serving 368

15 minutes in total

V Serves 2

1 heaped teaspoon chopped fresh thyme

300 g (10½ oz) portobello mushrooms,
*   sliced thickly*

2 garlic cloves, crushed

½ a loaf of ciabatta

410 g can cannellini beans in water

1 tablespoon half fat crème fraîche

50 g (1¾ oz) low fat soft cheese

1 teaspoon grainy mustard

½ teaspoon grated lemon zest

freshly ground black pepper

1 Reserve a few thyme leaves to garnish then place the rest in a lidded saucepan with the mushrooms, garlic, 2 tablespoons of water and a seasoning of black pepper. Cover and cook for 5 minutes until the mushrooms are juicy, then remove the lid and cook for 2–3 minutes until all the liquid has evaporated. Preheat the grill to medium.

2 Meanwhile, cut the ciabatta lengthwise then cut each half into two pieces. Toast under the grill until golden and crisp.

3 Tip the cannellini beans and their liquid into another saucepan and cook gently for 2–3 minutes until heated through. Drain the beans then use a hand blender to whizz to a purée with the crème fraiche, soft cheese, mustard and lemon zest.

4 Spoon the bean purée on top of the ciabatta toasts and pile the mushrooms on top. Serve straightaway, garnished with the reserved thyme leaves.

Try this

This recipe can also be served as a starter for four, serving one ciabatta toast per person, topped with the bean purée and mushrooms. Add a few mixed leaves as an accompaniment.

You can use this recipe as a guide for how to make a basic risotto, then vary it by adding different ingredients such as a mixture of mushrooms or grilled tomatoes.

Spring vegetable risotto

Calories per serving 422

10 minutes preparation

30 minutes cooking

V Serves 2

2 teaspoons low fat spread

1 leek, sliced

2 carrots, peeled and diced

400 ml (14 fl oz) vegetable stock

125 g (4½ oz) dried Arborio rice

100 ml (3½ fl oz) dry white wine

100 g (3½ oz) asparagus tips,
    chopped roughly

75 g (2¾ oz) frozen peas

2 tablespoons chopped fresh basil

15 g (½ oz) freshly grated vegetarian hard
    Italian cheese

1 Melt the low fat spread in a large lidded saucepan or frying pan. Add the leek, carrot and 2 tablespoons of the stock. Cover the pan and cook gently for 5 minutes.

2 Remove the lid, stir the rice in with the softened vegetables and cook for 1 minute, stirring, until the rice starts to look slightly translucent.

3 Add the wine to the pan and allow it to bubble until it is absorbed. Place a small lidded saucepan over a low heat, pour in the rest of the stock, cover and keep hot (barely simmering) while you make the risotto.

4 Add a third of the hot stock to the rice and vegetables and simmer gently until all the liquid has been absorbed. Repeat this process twice more until the rice is swollen, slightly sticky and tender, but still has a little bit of bite left to it. If the rice still seems too firm, add a little boiling water and cook for a couple of minutes more.

5 When the last of the stock has been added, fill the same pan with boiling water and return to the boil. Add the asparagus tips and peas and cook for 3 minutes until tender. Drain and refresh briefly by running under cold water, to stop the cooking process.

6 Stir the asparagus, peas, basil and hard Italian cheese into the finished risotto and serve in warmed bowls.

V Try this

For a mushroom risotto: replace the leek and carrot with a finely chopped onion in step 1. After cooking for 5 minutes, add 250 g (9 oz) chopped mixed mushrooms and cook for 3 minutes, then continue with step 2. Omit the asparagus tips, peas and basil.

This classic combination of tomatoes, spinach and cheese is usually prepared with tubes of cannelloni but pancakes make a delicious, light alternative.

Spinach and ricotta pancakes

Calories per serving 291

35 minutes to prepare

20 minutes cooking

V ✳ before oven cooking

Serves 4

1 x Perfect Pancakes recipe
(see page 26)
225 g (8 oz) fresh young leaf spinach
2 garlic cloves, crushed
125 g (4½ oz) ricotta cheese
100 g (3½ oz) low fat soft cheese
freshly grated nutmeg
25 g (1 oz) freshly grated vegetarian hard
Italian cheese
500 g carton passata with basil

1 Make the Perfect Pancakes following the recipe on page 26 and set aside.

2 Preheat the oven to Gas Mark 6/200°C/fan oven 180°C. Place the spinach and garlic in a large pan and cook, stirring, until the spinach wilts. Drain in a colander and press to extract most of the liquid then chop the spinach.

3 Mix the ricotta and soft cheese together with the spinach and a generous seasoning of nutmeg. Reserve 2 heaped teaspoons of the hard Italian cheese then mix the rest into the spinach and ricotta mixture.

4 Divide the spinach and ricotta mixture between the pancakes then roll up and place side by side in a baking dish. Pour the passata on top, scatter with the reserved hard Italian cheese and bake in the oven for 20 minutes until bubbling.

Cook's tip

Keen cooks can replace the passata with one recipe of Speedy Tomato Sauce (see page 19).

Cheat's tip

If you prefer, you can use frozen chopped spinach in step 2, cooking it from frozen and pressing out the excess liquid through a sieve rather than a colander.

Serve with a peppery salad of watercress, spinach and rocket leaves, scattered with half moons of thinly sliced cucumber and radishes.

Tomato and goat's cheese lasagne

Calories per serving 281

25 minutes to prepare

30 minutes cooking

V ✳ Serves 6

1 x Simple White Sauce recipe
    (see page 20)

9 sheets dried lasagne

100 ml (3½ fl oz) skimmed milk

500 g carton of passata

400 g can chopped tomatoes with herbs
    and garlic

20 g pack chopped fresh basil

100 g (3½ oz) individual goat's cheese,
    diced

25 g (1 oz) freshly grated vegetarian hard
    Italian cheese

1 Preheat the oven to Gas Mark 4/180°C/fan oven 160°C.

2 Make the Simple White Sauce, following the recipe on page 20, then add the milk to give a thinner consistency.

3 Spread a third of the white sauce over the base of a baking dish, measuring approximately 23 x 30 cm (9 x 12 inches) and add three sheets of lasagne.

4 Mix together the passata and canned tomatoes then stir in the basil. Add half of the tomato sauce and half of the goat's cheese to the baking dish then continue with layers of lasagne, the rest of the tomato sauce and goat's cheese, then a final layer of lasagne sheets.

5 Pour the remaining white sauce evenly over the lasagne and sprinkle the hard Italian cheese all over the top.

6 Bake in the oven for 30 minutes until the pasta is tender and the top has a golden brown crust.

Try this

Instead of the passata and canned tomatoes, you could use two quantities of the Speedy Tomato Sauce on page 19.

These cheesy parcels in filo pastry are the ideal make-ahead meal. They can be stored ready-made in the freezer and then baked in less than half an hour. Serve with sugar snap peas and Chantenay carrots.

Stilton stuffed mushrooms in filo

Calories per serving 303

20 minutes preparation

15 minutes cooking

V ✳ uncooked

Serves 4

4 large flat mushrooms

calorie controlled cooking spray

6 spring onions, chopped

150 g (5½ oz) mushrooms, chopped

2 garlic cloves, crushed

75 g (2¾ oz) fresh breadcrumbs

1 tablespoon chopped fresh thyme

100 g (3½ oz) baby leaf spinach

50 g (1¾ oz) Stilton, crumbled

25 g (1 oz) walnuts, chopped

4 x 45 g (1½ oz) sheets frozen filo,
    measuring 50 cm x 24 cm
    (20 x 9½ inches), defrosted

1 Preheat the oven to Gas Mark 6/200°C/fan oven 180°C. Remove the stalks from the flat mushrooms, chop up and set aside to use for the stuffing. Spray the flat mushrooms with a little cooking spray and place on a non stick baking tray, gill side up. Add 1 teaspoon water to each mushroom and bake in the oven for 10 minutes, turning over halfway through.

2 Meanwhile, to make the stuffing, spray a non stick frying pan with the cooking spray and fry the spring onions, chopped mushrooms and reserved mushroom stalks for 3–4 minutes. Add the garlic and cook for 1 minute more.

3 Tip the mushroom mixture into a bowl and mix with the breadcrumbs and thyme then divide the mixture between two bowls. Add the spinach to the frying pan and cook for 2 minutes or until wilted. Remove from the pan and chop finely. Stir the spinach, Stilton and walnuts into one bowl of the crumb mixture, for the stuffing.

4 Taking each sheet of filo in turn, spray it lightly with cooking spray then fold in half to make a square. Spoon a quarter of the mushroom and crumb mixture into the centre (the crumb mixture will absorb any juices from the mushroom, so the pastry doesn't go soggy) and place a flat mushroom on top. Pile a quarter of the spinach, Stilton and walnut stuffing on to the mushroom then fold in the corners of the pastry to seal in the mushroom. Spray each parcel with a little more cooking spray, place on a baking tray and cook for 15 minutes until crisp and golden brown.

Cook's tip

If you're making these parcels in advance and cooking them later, make sure that the mushrooms and the stuffing are both cool before you assemble the parcels, as otherwise the pastry may become soggy.

✳ **Freezer tip**

Freeze in step 4 once fully assembled. The parcels of mushrooms in filo can be cooked from frozen: cook at Gas Mark 4/180°C/fan oven 160°C for 25 minutes.

Sunflower seeds add a tasty crunch to the topping of this savoury crumble. Sugar snap peas and 150 g (5½ oz) boiled new potatoes per person would be a good side dish.

Mushroom, leek and chestnut crumble

Calories per serving 345

15 minutes preparation

15 minutes cooking

V ✳ before oven-cooking

Serves 2

2 leeks, sliced thickly

1 teaspoon chopped fresh rosemary
 (or ½ teaspoon dried)

200 ml (7 fl oz) vegetable stock

300 g (10½ oz) mushrooms, quartered

15 g (½ oz) plain flour

50 g (1¾ oz) low fat soft cheese

75 g (2¾ oz) cooked peeled chestnuts,
 chopped roughly

40 g (1½ oz) fresh breadcrumbs

25 g (1 oz) half fat mature cheese, grated

1 tablespoon sunflower seeds

1 Preheat the oven to Gas Mark 6/200°C/fan oven 180°C.

2 Place the leeks and rosemary in a lidded saucepan with 3 tablespoons of the stock, cover and cook for 3 minutes. Add the mushrooms plus 1 tablespoon stock, cover and cook for a further 3 minutes.

3 Stir the flour then gradually add the rest of the stock. Bring to a simmer, stirring, and cook for 2 minutes. Mix in the soft cheese to give a creamy sauce and stir in the chestnuts. Pour the mixture into two individual ovenproof dishes, or one slightly larger serving dish.

4 Mix the breadcrumbs, cheese and sunflower seeds together and press on top of the leek and mushroom mixture. Place on a baking tray and cook in the oven for 15 minutes until golden brown and bubbling.

Cook's tip

Cooked and peeled chestnuts can be bought ready-prepared, either in a can or sealed in a vacuum pack. When trying to track them down in the supermarket, you'll most likely find them next to the stuffing mixes or near the canned pulses.

Aubergine, feta and poppyseed tart

Calories per serving 267

40 minutes preparation + chilling

40 minutes cooking

V Serves 6

For the pastry

25 g (1 oz) poppy seeds

150 g (5½ oz) self-raising flour

75 g (2¾ oz) low fat spread

a pinch of salt

For the filling

2 onions, sliced

100 ml (3½ fl oz) vegetable stock

400 g can chopped tomatoes

1 garlic clove, crushed

1 teaspoon caster sugar

2 tablespoons chopped fresh basil,
    plus extra leaves to garnish

calorie controlled cooking spray

1 aubergine, cut into 8 mm (⅜ inch) slices

150 g (5½ oz) feta cheese, crumbled

1 Start by making the pastry. Toast the poppy seeds in a dry frying pan for 1–2 minutes until they smell nutty. Remove from the heat and cool. Reserve 1 teaspoon of the flour for rolling out then sift the remaining flour into a mixing bowl. Add the low fat spread then use an ordinary table knife to cut the spread into smaller pieces, mixing into the flour as you go. Next, using your fingertips, rub the two together until the mixture looks like crumbs. Stir in the poppy seeds and a pinch of salt then gradually add enough cold water to bring the pastry together, without making it sticky – you'll need about 2 tablespoons in total, but stop adding water as soon as the pastry starts to hold together in lumps (adding too much water makes it tough). The mixture will still look quite dry at this stage, but gently bring it together by hand and you will find that it should stick together in a ball, leaving the bowl clean. Wrap in cling film and chill for 30 minutes.

2 Place the onions in a lidded saucepan with the stock and cook, covered, for 10 minutes. Remove the lid. Cook, stirring for 2–3 minutes until starting to colour. Add the tomatoes, garlic and caster sugar then simmer for 10 minutes. Stir in the basil.

3 Spray the aubergine slices with the cooking spray and grill for 3–4 minutes on each side until lightly golden and soft. Set aside. Preheat the oven to Gas Mark 4/180°C/fan oven 160°C.

4 Dust the work surface with flour. Press down on the ball of pastry with a rolling pin to form it into a fat disc. Encourage it to form an even circular shape then start to roll the pastry out, rolling straight ahead of you then turning the pastry a quarter turn after each roll, rather than swivelling the rolling pin around as this stretches the pastry unevenly. Roll the pastry out to a 30 cm (12 inch) circle to line a 23 cm (9 inch) flan tin.

5 Carefully lift the pastry into the flan tin, using the rolling pin to help you. Press the pastry into the base and sides of the tin then roll the rolling pin straight across the top of the tin to trim off any excess pastry. Line the pastry case with foil.

6 Blind bake the tart case for 10 minutes until set then remove the foil and cook for a further 5 minutes until the pastry is lightly golden brown. Scatter half of the feta cheese in the base of the tart case then spoon the tomato and onion sauce on top. Cover the top of the tart with the aubergine slices, overlapping them, and scatter with the rest of the feta. Alternatively, put all the feta on top. Bake for 20–25 minutes, covering with foil if the aubergines are getting too dark.

7 Serve the tart warm or cold, garnished with the basil leaves.

A wonderfully aromatic rice dish with a curry sauce, you might like to serve this biryani with fine green beans and top with freshly chopped coriander.

Chick pea biryani with cashews

Calories per serving 394

5 minutes preparation

25 minutes cooking

V Serves 4

25 g (1 oz) cashews, chopped roughly

2 onions, sliced

700 ml (1¼ pints) vegetable stock

1 teaspoon cumin seeds

2 teaspoons medium curry powder

1 teaspoon garam masala

1 tablespoon sultanas

200 g (7 oz) dried basmati rice

400 g can chick peas in water, drained
   and rinsed

8 heaped teaspoons Bisto Chip Shop
   Curry Sauce granules (see Cheat's tip)

300 ml (10 fl oz) boiling water

1   Toast the cashews in a dry-frying pan for 3–4 minutes until golden. Set aside for the garnish.

2   Place the onions in a large lidded saucepan with 100 ml (3½ fl oz) of the stock, cover and cook for 5–6 minutes over a medium heat until translucent. Remove the lid, increase the heat and cook for 5 minutes, stirring occasionally, until starting to brown.

3   Add the cumin seeds, curry powder, garam masala and sultanas, plus the basmati rice. Cook for 1 minute, stirring, to bring out the flavours.

4   Mix in the chick peas and the rest of the stock. Bring to the boil, stir once then put the lid on the pan, reduce the heat to the lowest setting and cook undisturbed for 15 minutes, by which time the rice will be tender and have absorbed all the liquid. Scatter the cashews over the biryani.

5   Make up the curry sauce granules with boiling water following the packet instructions, and serve with the biryani.

Cook's tip

If you can't find the Chip Shop Curry Sauce Granules, serve with ½ x 500 g jar of medium curry sauce such as Homepride curry cook-in-sauce.

Cheat's tip

Keen cooks can replace the Chip Shop Curry Sauce Granules with two portions of home-made Curry Sauce (see page 18). Simply heat through and serve with the biryani.

Kosheri is a popular Egyptian street-food dish. It's a hearty rustic recipe made from very economical ingredients, comprising a mixture of lentils, aromatic rice and macaroni, served with a spicy tomato sauce and a topping of caramelised onions. It's one of those recipes in which the simplicity of the ingredients belies the complex and comforting flavours of the end result – simply delicious.

Kosheri

Calories per serving 400

15 minutes preparation

35 minutes cooking

V Serves 4

150 g (5½ oz) dried green lentils, rinsed

calorie controlled cooking spray

1 red chilli, de-seeded and diced

2 garlic cloves, crushed

1 teaspoon ground cumin

400 g can chopped tomatoes

1 tablespoon red wine vinegar

1 litre (1¾ pints) vegetable stock

2 onions, sliced

1 teaspoon olive oil

1 teaspoon light brown sugar

150 g (5½ oz) dried basmati rice

50 g (1¾ oz) dried macaroni

1 cinnamon stick

a kettleful of boiling water

1   Place the lentils in a small lidded saucepan, cover with cold water and bring to the boil. Cook briskly, uncovered, for 10 minutes then reduce the heat and simmer, covered, for 15 minutes or until tender but still whole. Don't over-cook or the lentils will start to collapse.

2   Meanwhile, make the spicy tomato sauce. Spray a lidded saucepan with the cooking spray and fry the chilli, garlic and cumin for 30 seconds then add the chopped tomatoes, vinegar and 175 ml (6 fl oz) of the stock. Bring to the boil and simmer, partially covered, for 20 minutes.

3   Next, cook the caramelised onions for the topping. Place the onions in a lidded non stick pan with 150 ml (5 fl oz) of the stock. Cook, covered, for 10 minutes until soft then remove the lid. Add the olive oil and sugar (these will both help the onions to caramelise), increase the heat and cook, stirring frequently, for 10 minutes or until sticky and dark brown. Keep a close eye on the onions towards the end of this time, to make sure that they aren't sticking to the pan or burning.

4   To cook the rice and pasta, bring the rest of the stock to the boil in a lidded saucepan, adding the cinnamon stick. Stir in both the rice and pasta and bring back to the boil together. Simmer briskly for 5 minutes then reduce the heat to low, cover and cook for 15 minutes without lifting the lid. By the end of this time, the rice and pasta should be tender and have absorbed all the liquid. Remove from the heat and set aside for 5 minutes, covered with a clean towel to absorb the steam and to allow the rice to fluff up. Discard the cinnamon stick then spoon the rice and pasta into four deep bowls.

5   Drain the lentils, and rinse briefly with some boiling water from the kettle. Drizzle over the spicy tomato sauce and serve topped with the lentils and caramelised onions.

Cheat's tip
Replace the dried lentils with a 410 g can of ready-cooked green lentils, drained. Simply heat through in their canning liquid until piping hot then rinse with boiling water before serving.

CHAPTER : 8

Everyday value

Everyone loves toad in the hole, and this recipe rings the changes by shaping the sausage meat into little balls to find within the crisp batter. Green cabbage and steamed carrots are ideal served alongside.

Sage and onion toad in the hole

Calories per serving 448
30 minutes preparation
30 minutes cooking
Serves 4

calorie controlled cooking spray
8 Weight Watchers Premium Pork
    Sausages, snipped in half
2 red onions, sliced
125 g (4½ oz) plain flour
1 tablespoon chopped fresh sage or
    1 teaspoon dried
2 eggs
300 ml (10 fl oz) skimmed milk
2 teaspoons sunflower oil
1 x Goes-with-Everything Gravy recipe
    (see page 16)
100 ml (3½ fl oz) vegetable stock
1 teaspoon light brown sugar
1 tablespoon balsamic vinegar
salt and freshly ground black pepper

1   Preheat the oven to Gas Mark 7/220°C/fan oven 200°C. Spray a solid roasting tin, measuring approximately 22 x 30 cm (8½ x 12 inches), with the cooking spray.

2   Squeeze the sausages out of their skins and roll each piece into a ball. Place in the roasting tin and scatter half the sliced onion around. Spray again with the cooking spray and roast in the oven for 7 minutes.

3   Meanwhile, make the batter. Sift the flour into a mixing bowl and stir in the sage and season. Make a well in the centre and add the eggs. Start to beat the eggs and flour together using a wire whisk, adding the milk gradually until you have a smooth batter.

4   When the 7 minutes is up, remove the roasting tin from the oven and stir the sausage balls and onions around to make sure that nothing is sticking to the tin. Add the oil to the roasting tin and heat on the hob for 30 seconds. Pour in the batter, then replace the tin in the centre of the oven and cook for 30 minutes until risen and crisp.

5   While the toad in the hole is cooking, make the Goes-with-Everything Gravy, following the recipe on page 16.

6   Place the rest of the onion in a lidded non stick saucepan with the stock and cook gently, covered, for 10 minutes until softened. Remove the lid, sprinkle in the sugar and increase the heat under the pan. Cook, stirring frequently, for 5 minutes or until the onions are caramelised and sticky. Add the balsamic vinegar then stir the onions into the gravy.

7   Serve the caramelised onion gravy with the toad in the hole.

V Try this
Use 8 Quorn sausages, cut in half.

A fabulous version of a takeaway favourite, accompanied by a creamy potato salad.

Crispy coated chicken with minted potato salad

Calories per serving 556

20 minutes preparation

40 minutes cooking

Serves 4

15 g (½ oz) plain flour

4 x 250 g (9 oz) skinless chicken legs
   (see Cook's tip about removing skin)

1 egg, beaten with 1 tablespoon water

75 g (2¾ oz) fresh breadcrumbs

½ teaspoon smoked paprika

½ teaspoon dried thyme or oregano

1 garlic clove, crushed

calorie controlled cooking spray

500 g (1 lb 2 oz) new potatoes,
   cut into chunky pieces

1 x Creamy Dressing recipe
   (see page 14)

1 red pepper, de-seeded and diced

¼ teaspoon ground cumin

2 teaspoons chopped fresh mint

freshly ground black pepper

1   Preheat the oven to Gas Mark 5/190°C/fan oven 170°C.

2   Season the flour with pepper then use to dust the chicken legs (this will help the egg cling in the next stage).

3   Dip each chicken leg in the egg mixture. Mix the breadcrumbs with the smoked paprika, thyme and garlic and spread out in a shallow dish. Press the egg-coated chicken in the flavoured crumbs, patting them on to form an even layer.

4   Arrange the chicken on a foil-lined baking tray and spray lightly with cooking spray. Bake in the oven for 40 minutes until golden brown and crisp.

5   Meanwhile, bring a pan of water to the boil. Add the potatoes, return to the boil and cook for 12–15 minutes until tender. Drain and leave to cool.

6   Make the Creamy Dressing, following the recipe on page 14. Mix the red pepper, ground cumin and mint into the dressing, then add the cooled potatoes. Serve with the crispy coated chicken.

Cook's tip

If you need to skin the chicken legs, the easiest way to do this is to use a piece of kitchen paper to grip the skin at the fat end of each leg then tug it down and off over the drumstick bone and discard.

Try this

You can also make this recipe with 4 x 150 g (5½ oz) skinless chicken breast fillets instead of the chicken legs. Cook at Gas Mark 6/200°C/fan oven 180°C for 20 minutes.

Another family classic, given a slight twist by using wholewheat penne and adding roasted cherry tomatoes which create delicious bursts of flavour as you bite into them. Serve with broccoli and cauliflower florets.

Roasted tomato 'macaroni' cheese

Calories per serving 378
20 minutes preparation
20 minutes cooking
Serves 4

350 g (12 oz) cherry tomatoes
calorie controlled cooking spray
1 teaspoon chopped fresh thyme
½ teaspoon caster sugar
250 g (9 oz) dried wholewheat penne or
    other pasta shape of your choice
40 g (1½ oz) cornflour
450 ml (16 fl oz) skimmed milk
1 bay leaf
40 g (1½ oz) half fat Cheddar cheese,
    grated
40 g (1½ oz) freshly grated Parmesan
    cheese
½ teaspoon Dijon mustard
15 g (½ oz) fresh breadcrumbs

1 Preheat the oven to Gas Mark 6/200°C/fan oven 180°C. Place the cherry tomatoes in a 20 cm (8 inches) square baking dish and spray with the cooking spray. Add the thyme and sugar and toss around to coat. Roast in the oven for 12–15 minutes until the skins start to split.

2 Meanwhile, bring a saucepan of water to the boil. Add the pasta and return to the boil. Cook for 10 minutes or until tender.

3 To make the cheese sauce, blend the cornflour with a little of the milk in a non stick saucepan, stirring until smooth. Gradually add the rest of the milk. Drop in the bay leaf and bring the sauce to the boil, stirring. Simmer for 2 minutes then remove from the heat and stir in the Cheddar cheese, 25 g (1 oz) of the Parmesan cheese and the Dijon mustard. Remove the bay leaf.

4 Drain the pasta and mix with the cheese sauce and tip into the baking dish on top of the roasted tomatoes. Gently mix together.

5 Stir the breadcrumbs and the rest of the Parmesan cheese together in a small bowl then sprinkle on top of the 'macaroni' cheese.

6 Bake in the oven for 20 minutes until crisp, golden brown and bubbling.

Meatloaf is a great family-pleaser and makes a pleasant change from the usual mince dishes such as bolognese and chilli.

Turkey and sweetcorn meatloaf with lemon sauce

Calories per serving 270

15 minutes preparation

25 minutes cooking

✳ Serves 4

75 g (2¾ oz) fresh breadcrumbs

2 tablespoons skimmed milk

500 g (1 lb 2 oz) turkey mince

6 spring onions, chopped

1 egg white, beaten

198g can sweetcorn, drained

2 teaspoons chopped fresh thyme

15 g (½ oz) Parmesan cheese

grated zest and juice of ½ a small lemon

15 g (½ oz) cornflour

250 ml (9 fl oz) chicken stock

1 Preheat the oven to Gas Mark 4/180°C/fan oven 160°C. Line a baking tray with baking parchment.

2 Mix the breadcrumbs and milk together in a mixing bowl and then add the turkey mince, two thirds of the spring onions, the egg white, sweetcorn, thyme, Parmesan cheese and half the lemon zest. Mix together well then form into a loaf shape about 20 cm (8 inches) long on the baking tray.

3 Bake in the oven for 25 minutes, or until the juices run clear when the middle of the meatloaf is pierced with a skewer, to ensure it is cooked all the way through.

4 Meanwhile, blend the cornflour and lemon juice in a non stick saucepan. Gradually mix in the stock then add the rest of the spring onions and lemon zest. Bring to the boil, stirring, and then simmer for 2 minutes.

5 Slice the meatloaf and serve with the lemon sauce.

A family favourite with a spicy twist. Runner beans make a great side dish.

Indian shepherd's pie

Calories per serving 325

30 minutes preparation

25 minutes cooking

V ✳ Serves 6

1 onion, chopped finely

350 ml (12 fl oz) vegetable stock

2 tablespoons medium curry powder

500 g (1 lb 2 oz) Quorn mince

50 g (1¾ oz) dried red lentils, rinsed

400 g can chopped tomatoes

1.25 kg (2 lb 12 oz) potatoes, peeled and
   chopped roughly

100 ml (3½ fl oz) skimmed milk

1 tablespoon cumin seeds, toasted

150 g (5½ oz) frozen peas

1   Preheat the oven to Gas Mark 6/200°C/fan oven 180°C.

2   Put the onion and 100 ml (3½ fl oz) of the stock in a large, lidded non stick saucepan. Cover and cook for 6 minutes until the onion is tender. Add the curry powder and cook for 1 minute then mix in the Quorn mince, lentils, tomatoes and remaining stock. Bring to the boil, cover and simmer for 15 minutes.

3   Meanwhile, bring a large saucepan of water to the boil, add the potatoes and return to the boil. Cook for 15–18 minutes until tender. Drain and mash with the milk and the cumin seeds.

4   Mix the peas into the Quorn and lentil mixture then transfer to a large baking dish. Spoon the mashed potato over the top of the mince. Bake in the oven for 20–25 minutes until the shepherd's pie has a golden brown crust and is bubbling.

✳ Cook's tip

If you don't need to serve six people at one meal, you can prepare the shepherd's pie in individual dishes instead. These can be frozen, covered well with cling film, but defrost before cooking.

Try this

Try substituting lamb mince for the Quorn mince. In step 2, instead of cooking the onion in stock, brown the mince and onion in a large, lidded, non stick frying pan for 8–10 minutes before adding the curry powder. Add only 250 ml (9 fl oz) stock with the lentils and tomatoes.

Pot-roasting involves cooking the meat in a sealed pot on a base of vegetables, which help to flavour the meat as it cooks to complete tenderness.

Pot roast beef with thyme dumplings

Calories per serving 473
20 minutes preparation
1 hour 20 minutes cooking
Serves 4

calorie controlled cooking spray
750 g (1 lb 10 oz) joint lean rolled
   silverside of beef
2 onions, cut into wedges
4 carrots, peeled and chopped roughly
4 whole garlic cloves, peeled
125 ml (4 fl oz) red wine
125 ml (4 fl oz) beef stock
4 tomatoes, quartered
2 fresh thyme sprigs, plus 2 teaspoons
   chopped fresh thyme
100 g (3½ oz) self raising flour
50 g (1¾ oz) low fat spread

1 Preheat the oven to Gas Mark 2/150°C/fan oven 130°C. Heat a lidded flameproof casserole, spray lightly with the cooking spray and brown the beef for 5 minutes over a high heat, turning to colour all sides. Remove to a plate.

2 Add the onions, carrots and garlic to the casserole and brown for 3–4 minutes then add the wine, stock, tomatoes and thyme sprigs. Snuggle the beef in amongst the vegetables then cover and cook in the oven for 1 hour.

3 5 minutes before the hour is up, place the flour and low fat spread in a mixing bowl and rub together until the mixture looks like breadcrumbs. Stir in the chopped thyme then add just enough cold water to bring the mixture together as a soft but not sticky dough. Shape into eight dumplings then nestle these around the beef in the casserole.

4 Put the lid back on the casserole and then return to the oven for 20 minutes.

5 Lift the beef and dumplings out to a serving dish, along with roughly two thirds of the vegetables from the sauce, using a draining spoon. Use a hand blender to purée the rest of the vegetables and cooking liquid to make a thickened gravy.

6 Carve the beef into slices and serve a quarter of the meat per person, accompanied by the vegetables, sauce and dumplings.

Cook's tips
If you prefer not to use wine, simply increase the amount of beef stock to 250 ml (9 fl oz).

To make peeling the garlic cloves easier, press down on each clove with the flat of a kitchen knife to loosen the skin, them remove it and discard.

Serve these succulent little patties in sweet chilli sauce with a pile of tenderstem broccoli.

Asian pork patties with coriander rice

Calories per serving 404

30 minutes in total

❄ for uncooked patties only

Serves 4

500 g (1 lb 2 oz) extra lean pork mince
50 g (1¾ oz) fresh breadcrumbs
2.5 cm (1 inch) fresh root ginger, grated
½ red chilli, de-seeded and diced
2 garlic cloves, crushed
grated zest of ½ a lime
4 tablespoons chopped fresh coriander
calorie controlled cooking spray
200 g (7 oz) dried Jasmine rice
450 ml (16 fl oz) boiling water

For the sauce

3 tablespoons Thai sweet chilli sauce
1 tablespoon soy sauce
1 teaspoon light brown sugar
juice of ½ a lime

1 Mix together the pork mince, breadcrumbs, ginger, chilli, garlic, lime zest and half of the coriander. Shape into 20 patties, each measuring about 5 cm (2 inches) in diameter.

2 Heat a large non stick frying pan and spray with the cooking spray. Add the patties and cook for 5 minutes on each side, until browned and cooked through.

3 Meanwhile, place the rice and boiling water in a lidded saucepan. Return to the boil, stir once to separate the grains then reduce the heat to low, cover and cook for 15 minutes, without lifting the lid.

4 To make the sauce, mix the sweet chilli sauce, soy sauce and sugar together with 125 ml (4 fl oz) water and the lime juice. Pour this sauce into the frying pan and cook for 2 minutes, turning the patties over to glaze.

5 Stir the coriander into the Jasmine rice and serve with the pork patties, drizzled with the pan juices.

Try this
You can also make this recipe with 500 g (1 lb 2 oz) turkey mince, if you prefer.

This is incredibly delicious topped with ½ tablespoon half fat crème fraîche per person.

Pepperpot beef

Calories per serving 240

20 minutes preparation

1½ hours cooking

❋ Serves 6

15 g (½ oz) plain flour

½ teaspoon ground ginger

500 g (1 lb 2 oz) lean diced
    casserole steak

calorie controlled cooking spray

2 x 400 g cans chopped tomatoes

1 tablespoon light brown soft sugar

1 tablespoon red wine vinegar

2 garlic cloves, crushed

2 teaspoons Worcestershire sauce

1–2 teaspoons hot chilli pepper sauce

410 g can kidney beans in water,
    rinsed and drained

1 pack of 3 mixed peppers, de-seeded
    and diced

1 Preheat the oven to Gas Mark 2/150°C/fan oven 130°C. Mix the flour and ginger together and toss the beef in the mixture to coat.

2 Heat a large non stick frying pan, spray lightly with the cooking spray and add the beef in batches. Brown for 4–5 minutes, turning over halfway through, then remove to a plate and repeat with the remaining meat. Don't overcrowd the pan or the meat will steam rather than brown.

3 Meanwhile, place the tomatoes, sugar, vinegar, garlic, Worcestershire sauce and chilli pepper sauce in a lidded flameproof casserole. Bring to the boil, add the beef and bring back to a simmer. Place a lid on the casserole and cook in the oven for 1 hour.

4 Stir the beans and peppers into the casserole and cook for a further 30 minutes.

5 Ladle into bowls to serve.

Cook's tip

When browning meat, don't try to turn it too soon. When you first add the meat to the hot frying pan it will stick to the pan, but as it browns and forms a crust it will release itself from the pan.

Cheat's tip

Replace the fresh peppers with 300 g (10½ oz) frozen sliced peppers in step 4, to cut down on preparation time.

Coating the meat in spiced flour and then browning it well adds colour and a delicious depth of flavour to the stew.

A deliciously different stew with a hint of sweetness from the parsnips and orange. Bake a 225 g (8 oz) potato per person and serve with green cabbage.

Autumnal chicken stew

Calories per serving 188

20 minutes preparation

45 minutes cooking

❄ Serves 6

500 g (1 lb 2 oz) skinless boneless
    chicken thigh fillets, each cut into four
calorie controlled cooking spray
1 onion, chopped roughly
3 carrots, peeled and sliced thickly
2 parsnips, peeled and cut
    into chunks
200 g (7 oz) mushrooms, chopped roughly
½ tablespoon plain flour
450 ml (16 fl oz) chicken stock
1 tablespoon chopped fresh thyme
grated zest and juice of ½ a small orange
100 g (3½ oz) cooked, peeled chestnuts

1 Heat a non stick frying pan over a high heat, add the chicken pieces (no need to use any cooking spray) and brown for 8 minutes, stirring occasionally to colour evenly.

2 Meanwhile, heat a lidded, flameproof casserole dish, spray with the cooking spray, add the onions and cook for 5 minutes over a high heat. Add the carrots, parsnips and mushrooms and cook for 2 minutes more.

3 Stir the flour in with the chicken, mixing well. Gradually add the stock plus the thyme, orange zest and juice. Pour the mixture into the casserole with the vegetables and add the chestnuts. Bring to a simmer, cover and cook gently for 45 minutes until the chicken and vegetables are tender.

4 Divide the chicken and vegetables between six warmed plates to serve.

A complete meal-in-a-bowl, this is a cross between a stew and a hearty soup and is best eaten with a spoon.

Fisherman's stew

Calories per serving 285
10 minutes preparation
30 minutes cooking
Serves 2

½ an orange
a pinch of saffron
calorie controlled cooking spray
1 yellow pepper, de-seeded and sliced
1 garlic clove, sliced
400 g can cherry tomatoes
1 teaspoon caster sugar
125 ml (4 fl oz) vegetable stock
175 g (6 oz) new potatoes,
    sliced 5 mm (½ inch) thick
200 g (7 oz) frozen seafood mix, defrosted
½ tablespoon cornflour

1   Pare three strips of zest from the orange using a vegetable peeler, and squeeze out the juice. Add the saffron to the orange juice and leave to soak.
2   Heat a large lidded saucepan over a medium heat and spray with the cooking spray. Add the pepper and garlic and stir-fry for 3 minutes.
3   Add the saffron and orange juice, the cherry tomatoes, caster sugar, stock and new potatoes, plus the pared orange zest. Bring to the boil, cover and simmer for 20 minutes or until the potatoes are tender.
4   Add the seafood mix and simmer for 5–8 minutes or until the seafood is piping hot.
5   Blend the cornflour with 2 tablespoons cold water then add to the pan and cook, stirring, until the sauce has thickened.
6   Ladle into bowls to serve.

A scrumptious savoury version of bread and butter pudding, this makes good use of leftovers. Serve with baby corn and sugar snap peas.

Ham and cheese bread pudding

Calories per serving 361
10 minutes preparation
30 minutes cooking
Serves 2

2 eggs
250 ml (9 fl oz) skimmed milk
5 slices calorie controlled bread, quartered
75 g (2¾ oz) premium ham, chopped
50 g (1¾ oz) half fat mature cheese, grated
6 cherry tomatoes, halved

1   Preheat the oven to Gas Mark 4/180°C/fan oven 160°C.
2   Beat the eggs with the milk in a shallow dish. Dip half of the pieces of bread in the mixture and place in the base of a baking dish. Scatter over half of the ham and cheese.
3   Repeat with the rest of the bread, again dipping it in the egg mixture, then add the rest of the ham and the tomatoes.
4   Pour in the egg mixture left in the dish then scatter the remaining cheese on top.
5   Bake in the oven for 30 minutes until puffy, firm and richly golden brown.

V Try this
Replace the ham with the same amount of Quorn Deli Ham slices.

This is sure to be a crowd pleaser and you can adjust the chilli content to suit your family's taste. Serve with a crisp leaf salad, mixed with carrot ribbons (pared from a raw carrot using a vegetable peeler).

Chunky sausage pasta bake

Calories per serving 424

20 minutes preparation

20 minutes cooking

Serves 4

1 x Speedy Tomato Sauce recipe
    (see page 19 and Cheat's tip)
200 g (7 oz) dried penne
calorie controlled cooking spray
6 Quorn sausages, chopped
2 onions, chopped roughly
2 teaspoon chopped fresh rosemary
    or 1 teaspoon dried
a pinch of dried chilli flakes
150 ml (5 fl oz) vegetable stock
125 g (4½ oz) light mozzarella cheese,
    drained and diced
25 g (1 oz) freshly grated Parmesan
    cheese

1   Make the Speedy Tomato Sauce, following the recipe on page 19.

2   Preheat the oven to Gas Mark 6/200°C/fan oven 180°C. Bring a saucepan of water to the boil, add the penne and return to the boil. Cook for 9 minutes, or 1 minute less than indicated by the packet instructions, so that the pasta is tender but still retains a little bite.

3   Meanwhile, heat a non stick frying pan, spray with cooking spray and fry the sausage chunks and onion with the rosemary and chilli for 5–6 minutes over a medium heat until starting to colour.

4   Drain the pasta and mix with the sausage mixture, the tomato sauce and the stock. Transfer to an ovenproof dish and scatter the mozzarella and Parmesan cheese on top.

5   Bake in the oven for 20 minutes until bubbling, with a golden cheesy crust.

Try this

If you prefer, use 6 Weight Watchers Premium Pork Sausages, snipped into chunks using kitchen scissors.

Cheat's tip

Instead of the Speedy Tomato Sauce, you could use a 350 g jar of low fat tomato pasta sauce.

Braised with aromatic ingredients such as ginger, star anise and cloves, the ham becomes both beautifully succulent and delicately flavoured as it cooks, then the broth is used to cook the accompanying vegetables to maximise the flavour. If you aren't planning on serving six people, any leftover ham is wonderful in a sandwich.

Aromatic braised ham

Calories per serving 390

10 minutes preparation

1½ hours cooking

Serves 6

750 g (1 lb 10 oz) unsmoked gammon joint

2.5 cm (1 inch) fresh root ginger, sliced

1 garlic clove, sliced

1 star anise

6 cloves

1 tomato, roughly chopped

4 spring onions

15 g (½ oz) sesame seeds

300 g (10½ oz) dried Jasmine rice

750 ml (1¼ pints) boiling water

150 g (5½ oz) tenderstem broccoli

2 pak choi, cut into 12 wedges

1   Place the gammon joint in a large lidded saucepan or casserole, along with the ginger, garlic, star anise, cloves and tomato. Roughly chop the white parts of the spring onions and add to the pan. Slice the green parts and reserve for later.

2   Add 2 litres (3½ pints) cold water, or enough to just cover the gammon. Bring to the boil, skim off any scum, cover and then simmer gently for 1 hour.

3   About 5 minutes before the ham is done, cook the rice. First dry-fry the sesame seeds in a large lidded saucepan for about 2 minutes or until golden. Add the rice and boiling water to the pan, bring back to the boil then stir once to separate the grains, cover and reduce the heat to low. Cook for 15 minutes, without lifting the lid. By the end of this time the rice should have absorbed all the liquid and be cooked through. Jasmine rice naturally has a slightly sticky texture, so don't be worried that the grains aren't completely separate.

4   When the ham is cooked, lift it out of the cooking broth and keep warm while you cook the vegetables. Discard the flavourings from the cooking broth and bring to the boil. Add the broccoli, return to the boil and cook uncovered for 3 minutes until tender. Lift out with a draining spoon and keep in a warmed serving dish.

5   Bring the broth back to the boil, add the wedges of pak choi to the pan, cover and cook for 2–3 minutes until tender. Remove to the same serving dish as the broccoli. Add the chopped spring onion greens to the cooking broth.

6   To serve, cut the ham into thin slices and divide between the plates. Place in a deep bowl, add some broccoli and pak choi then ladle on some of the aromatic cooking broth. Serve with the sesame rice.

This fabulously fragrant way to cook mussels is a real treat if you love shellfish. Serve with a 40 g (1½ oz) chunk of crusty French bread to dip into the lovely cooking juices.

Thai mussel pot

Calories per serving 576

15 minutes in total

Serves 1

500 g (1 lb 2 oz) fresh mussels in the shell

¼ red chilli, de-seeded and sliced

½ stalk lemongrass, crushed

1 garlic clove, sliced

1 cm (½ inch) fresh root ginger,
    cut into matchsticks

100 ml (3½ fl oz) reduced fat
    coconut milk

1 teaspoon light brown sugar

grated zest and juice of ½ a lime

2 tablespoons chopped fresh coriander

1   To prepare the mussels, place them in a sink full of cold water, scrub to remove any external dirt then pull out the hairy 'beards' or threads. If any mussels are open, give them a sharp tap on the edge of the sink, and if this doesn't make them close, discard, as the mussel is dead (see the step-by-step photo opposite, top left: the mussels on the left are open and need to be discarded; those on the right and closed and are fine).

2   Place the chilli, lemongrass, garlic, ginger, coconut milk, sugar, lime zest and juice in a large lidded saucepan. Bring to the boil then tip the prepared mussels into the pan. Cover and cook over a medium heat for 5 minutes. Shake the pan vigorously a couple of times to make sure that all the mussels come into contact with the hot liquid.

3   The mussels should now be cooked, and all of them should have opened. If any remain closed, discard these. Tip the mussels and their aromatic cooking juices into a deep bowl and scatter thickly with coriander. Serve straightaway, making sure that you have a spoon to scoop up the delicious liquid, and a spare plate or bowl for the discarded shells as you eat.

Cook's tip
The leftover coconut milk from a 400 ml tin can be frozen in handy 100 ml (3½ fl oz) portions, ready for the next time you make this recipe or for making the Quick Vietnamese Curry Noodles on page 100.

It's best to ladle this colourful casserole into deep plates or bowls, to make the most of the delicious sauce. Sugar snap peas would go well on the side.

One pot spring lamb casserole

Calories per serving 216

20 minutes preparation

1 hour cooking

Serves 6

calorie controlled cooking spray

500 g (1 lb 2 oz) lean diced lamb

12 shallots, peeled

300 g (10½ oz) Chantenay carrots,
    trimmed and halved lengthways

½ tablespoon plain flour

300 g (10½ oz) small new potatoes,
    halved

400 g can chopped tomatoes

1 heaped teaspoon clear honey

400 ml (14 fl oz) vegetable stock

2 tablespoons chopped fresh mint

100 g (3½ oz) frozen soya beans

1   Preheat the oven to Gas Mark 2/150°C/fan oven 130°C. Spray a lidded flameproof casserole dish with the cooking spray and brown the lamb in two batches, removing to a plate when browned.

2   Tip the shallots and carrots into the casserole dish and cook for 3 minutes until lightly coloured. Return the lamb to the casserole and stir in the flour. Add the potatoes, tomatoes, honey, stock and half the mint. Bring to a simmer, cover and cook in the oven for 55 minutes.

3   Mix the soya beans into the casserole and return to the oven for 5 minutes. Stir in the rest of the mint just before serving.

Cook's tips

To make it easier to peel the shallots, place them in a bowl and cover with boiling water. Leave to stand for 4–5 minutes then drain. Trim off the top and base then the skins will peel off easily.

If you don't want to use the oven, you can also cook this casserole on the hob for the same length of time. Just make sure that it cooks at a gentle simmer – when you lift the lid, there should only be a few bubbles. If the heat is too high, the meat may become tough.

A tasty all-in-one traybake that can be prepared in just a few minutes, then left to cook in the oven while you get on with something else. Delicious with steamed broccoli.

Italian chicken braise

Calories per serving 494

10 minutes preparation

1 hour cooking

Serves 4

600 g (1 lb 5 oz) potatoes, cut into
    wedges

1 garlic bulb, separated into cloves

1 fennel bulb, cut into wedges

calorie controlled cooking spray

4 x 250 g (9 oz) skinless chicken legs
    (see Cook's tip about removing skin)

4 plum tomatoes, cut into wedges

200 ml (7 fl oz) chicken stock

1 Preheat the oven to Gas Mark 7/220°C/fan oven 200°C.

2 Toss the potato wedges, garlic cloves and fennel together in a large roasting tin and spray lightly with the cooking spray. Roast in the oven for an initial 15 minutes or until starting to brown.

3 Heat a non stick frying pan over a high heat, spray lightly with the cooking spray then brown the chicken legs for 5 minutes, turning once.

4 Mix the tomatoes in with the vegetables in the roasting tin then nestle the chicken legs in amongst them. Pour in the chicken stock then cover the tray with foil, folding it around the edges of the tray. Reduce the oven temperature to Gas Mark 4/180°C/fan oven 160°C and cook for 40 minutes. The vegetables should be tender, and the chicken legs cooked through but still juicy. Serve on warmed plates.

Cook's tip

If you buy chicken legs with skin, the easiest way to skin them is to grip the skin at the fat end of each leg and then tug it down and off over the drumstick bone and discard.

Try this

If you'd rather make this with 4 x 150 g (5½ oz) skinless boneless chicken breasts, they won't need as much cooking time. Add the tomatoes to the other vegetables as in the main recipe, and cook together for 20 minutes at the reduced oven temperature, then add the browned chicken breasts and cook for a further 20 minutes.

Items on Loan

Library name: Derry
Central Library
User name: Mr Lawrence
Devine

Author: Burnett-Hall,
Tamsin,
Title: Weight Watchers the
complete kitchen
Item ID: C900994128
Date due: 27/4/2019,23:59
Date charged: 6/4/2019,
11:28

Libraries NI
****
Make your life easier
****
Email notifications are sent
two days before item due
dates
Ask staff to sign up for
Email

A fantastic store cupboard recipe, this pilaff is ideal for those days when you've practically run out of any fresh ingredients but haven't got time to get to the shops.

Pea and tuna pilaff

Calories per serving 426

15 minutes preparation

30 minutes cooking

Serves 2

calorie controlled cooking spray

1 onion, chopped finely

2 teaspoons medium curry powder

½ teaspoon cumin seeds

100 g (3½ oz) dried brown basmati rice

250 ml (9 fl oz) vegetable stock

2 eggs

100 g (3½ oz) frozen peas

185 g can tuna in spring water, drained

a squeeze of lemon juice

2 tablespoons chopped fresh coriander

1 Spray a large lidded saucepan with cooking spray and brown the onion for 4 minutes. Add the curry powder, cumin seeds and rice and cook, stirring, for 1 minute, to bring out the flavour of the spices.

2 Add the vegetable stock and bring to the boil. Stir the rice once to separate the grains, cover with a lid and reduce the heat to low. Cook for 25 minutes without lifting the lid.

3 Meanwhile, place the eggs in a small saucepan of cold water. Bring to the boil and simmer for 6 minutes. Drain and cool under cold running water (this stops a dark ring forming around the yolk). Peel the egg and chop it roughly.

4 Stir the peas and tuna into the rice then cook for 5 minutes more.

5 Gently mix the chopped egg and the lemon juice into the pilaff and serve scattered with coriander.

Cook's tip

It's well worth keeping a pot of ready-chopped coriander in the freezer to add as a flavoursome garnish to lift the whole dish, since fresh coriander doesn't keep for very long in the fridge.

Rice is the perfect accompaniment to these fragrant meatballs. Serve 60 g (2 oz) dried brown rice per person, cooked according to the pack instructions, and accompany with lightly cooked fine green beans or runner beans.

Turkish lamb kofte with sour cherries

Calories per serving 275

15 minutes preparation

45 minutes cooking

✱ excluding yogurt garnish

Serves 6

500 g (1 lb 2 oz) lean lamb mince

2 onions, one grated, one sliced thinly

60 g (2 oz) fresh breadcrumbs

100 ml (3½ fl oz) skimmed milk
    + 3 tablespoons

¼ teaspoon cayenne pepper

1 teaspoon ground cinnamon

2 teaspoons ground cumin

1 rounded tablespoon plain flour

600 ml (20 fl oz) vegetable stock

1 tablespoon lemon juice

1 heaped teaspoon clear honey

75 g (2¾ oz) dried sour cherries

200 g (7 oz) fresh cherries, stoned,
    or a 425 g can cherries in natural
    juice, drained

150 g (5½ oz) 0% fat Greek yogurt

3 tablespoons chopped fresh parsley

1   Place the lamb mince, grated onion, breadcrumbs, 100 ml (3½ fl oz) milk, cayenne pepper and half each of the cinnamon and cumin in a food processor or mixer and blend for 2 minutes or until light and smooth in texture.

2   Using wet hands, so that the mixture doesn't stick to you, shape into 36 small meatballs, or kofte, flattening each one slightly.

3   Heat a large non stick frying pan over a medium heat and dry-fry the kofte in two batches, for 2 minutes on each side until browned. Remove to a plate when they are ready.

4   Meanwhile, cook the sliced onion in 100 ml (3½ fl oz) of the stock in a lidded casserole for 8 minutes until soft. Remove the lid and cook for 2–3 minutes until the liquid has evaporated and the onions are sweet and translucent. Stir in the flour and the rest of the cinnamon and cumin. Cook for 1 minute, stirring, to bring out the flavours. Gradually add the stock, followed by the lemon juice, honey and dried cherries. Add the browned kofte and bring to a simmer. Cover and cook for 40 minutes.

5   Stir the fresh or canned cherries into the casserole and heat through for 5 minutes.

6   Thin down the yogurt with the 3 tablespoons skimmed milk then drizzle this over the kofte in their sauce. Serve sprinkled with the chopped parsley.

Cook's tip

If you don't have a food processor or mixer to make the meatballs you can simply beat the mixture well with a wooden spoon in a mixing bowl.

CHAPTER : 9

Sweet
endings

These easy scones can be knocked up in a moment if you've got friends popping in for tea. Any leftovers freeze very well, sealed in a plastic food bag, ready for next time.

Simple sultana scones

Calories per serving 97

10 minutes preparation

15 minutes cooking

V ✳ Makes 12

225 g (8 oz) self-raising flour

25 g (1 oz) low fat spread

25 g (1 oz) caster sugar

40 g (1½ oz) sultanas

150 g (5½ oz) virtually fat-free
    plain yogurt

2 teaspoons skimmed milk

1   Preheat the oven to Gas Mark 6/200°C/fan oven 180°C. Reserve 2 teaspoons of the flour for rolling (use a little to lightly dust on to a baking tray), then sift the rest into a mixing bowl. Rub the low fat spread into the flour until the mixture looks a bit like breadcrumbs, lifting your fingers up high as you rub the fat and flour together to incorporate as much air as possible.

2   Stir in the sugar and sultanas. Next stir in the yogurt, using a table knife, mixing to give a soft but not sticky dough that leaves the bowl clean. Add a little cold water to bring the dough together if it seems too dry and isn't clinging together.

3   Dust the work surface with the reserved flour and pat the dough out by hand to a thickness of 2.5 cm (1 inch). Use a 5 cm (2 inches) diameter cutter to stamp out the scone rounds. There will be plenty of trimmings left from the first cutting out, ready to pat out again and stamp out further rounds, until you have a total of 12 scones.

4   Place on the flour-dusted tray then brush the tops of the scones with the milk. Make sure that the milk doesn't drip down the sides of the scones too much, as this can stop them from rising.

5   Bake in the oven for 12–15 minutes until risen and golden brown. Cool slightly on a wire rack before serving.

Cook's tip

If you don't have a cutter, simply pat the dough out to a rectangle then cut into 12 small squares using a knife. Alternatively, cut into six larger squares then cut each one in half diagonally to make 12 triangular scones.

Try this

For plain sweet scones: make the recipe as above, but leave out the sultanas.

For savoury cheese scones: omit the sugar and sultanas from the recipe above and replace with ½ teaspoon Dijon mustard plus 40 g (½ oz) half fat mature cheese, grated finely. If you like, you can add just half of the cheese to the scone mixture then press the rest on to the top of the milk-brushed scones before baking, to give a lovely cheesy crust.

A great pud to prepare in advance, as all the elements can be made ahead of time.

A delectable cookie for the biscuit tin, this treat is lovely with a cup of tea or coffee.

Pancakes with baked plums

Calories per serving 242

30 minutes preparation

25 minutes cooking

V Serves 4

8 plums, halved and stoned

150 ml (5 fl oz) light cranberry juice

½ teaspoon mixed spice

25 g (1 oz) caster sugar

1 x Perfect Pancakes recipe
    (see page 26)

150 g pot 0% Greek yogurt

1 Preheat the oven to Gas Mark 6/200°C/fan oven 180°C. Place the halved plums in a baking dish and pour the cranberry juice all over them. Stir the mixed spice and sugar together and sprinkle over the plums.

2 Bake in the oven for 25 minutes, basting the plums with the cooking juices a couple of times, until they are tender. Serve them warm or at room temperature.

3 While the plums are baking, make the Perfect Pancakes, following the recipe on page 26.

4 Spread each pancake with a tablespoon of the yogurt then fold into quarters. Serve two pancakes per person with four plum halves and spoon over some of the juice. Accompany with the rest of the yogurt.

Cook's tip

Try the plums on their own.

Flapjack cookies

Calories per serving 67

10 minutes preparation

10 minutes cooking

V Makes 16

calorie controlled cooking spray

75 g (2¾ oz) low fat spread

1 tablespoon golden syrup

½ teaspoon bicarbonate of soda

1 tablespoon boiling water

50 g (1¾ oz) plain flour

100 g (3½ oz) porridge oats

40 g (1½ oz) granulated sugar

1 Preheat the oven to Gas Mark 4/180°C/fan oven 160°C. Lightly spray two baking trays with cooking spray.

2 Melt the low fat spread and golden syrup in a non stick saucepan. Dissolve the bicarbonate of soda in the boiling water then tip this into the pan, causing the mixture to foam slightly.

3 Mix in the flour, oats and sugar. Stir until well combined.

4 Use a tablespoon measure to dollop spoonfuls of the mixture on to the prepared trays – you should get a total of sixteen cookies. Flatten the cookies with the back of a spoon, and make sure that they have some room to spread.

5 Bake in the oven for about 8 minutes until golden brown – you will probably need to swap the trays over after 5 minutes. Keep a close eye on the cookies in the final minutes as the colour will change rapidly.

6 Cool the cookies on the trays for 5 minutes so they firm up slightly. Transfer to a wire rack to cool. Store in an airtight container for up to a week, although the cookies will lose some crispness over time.

Muffins are always popular for a mid-morning snack and the blueberries in these ones make them deliciously moist.

Blueberry muffins

Calories per serving 136

10 minutes preparation

20 minutes cooking

V ✳ Makes 12

250 g (9 oz) self-raising flour

1 teaspoon bicarbonate of soda

grated zest of ½ a lemon

75 g (2¾ oz) caster sugar

1 egg, beaten

250 ml (9 fl oz) buttermilk (see Cook's tip)

50 g (1¾ oz) low fat spread, melted

150 g (5½ oz) blueberries

1 teaspoon demerara sugar

1 Preheat the oven to Gas Mark 6/200°C/fan oven 180°C and line a 12-hole muffin tin with paper muffin cases.

2 Sift the flour and bicarbonate of soda into a mixing bowl and stir in the lemon zest and caster sugar.

3 In a separate bowl, or a jug, combine the egg, buttermilk and melted spread. Pour this into the bowl of dry ingredients and use a large spoon to stir and combine. Mix only until the ingredients are just mixed; the muffin mixture should still look rather lumpy. If it is mixed until completely smooth (as is normal for other cake mixtures) it will result in tough rubbery muffins.

4 Quickly stir the blueberries into the muffin mixture then divide between the paper muffin cases. Sprinkle the demerara sugar on top then bake in the oven for 20 minutes until risen, golden brown and firm to the touch.

5 Cool on a wire rack before eating. Muffins are best eaten on the day of baking, although they can be stored in an airtight container for up to two days. However, they also freeze extremely well, sealed inside plastic food bags.

Cook's tip

You can use either fresh or frozen blueberries in this recipe. If you opt for frozen, add them to the muffin mixture still in their frozen state; if you defrost them first they will soften and burst, turning the muffins an unappetising greyish-purple.

Try this

If you can't get hold of buttermilk, replace it with a mixture of 100 g (3½ oz) virtually fat-free plain yogurt plus 4 tablespoons skimmed milk.

This recipe makes scrumptious little squares of spiced apple cake, studded with cranberries. Individual pieces can be wrapped and frozen very successfully.

Apple and cranberry traybake squares

Calories per serving 97

15 minutes preparation

30 minutes cooking

V ✽ Makes 16 small squares

50 g (1¾ oz) caster sugar

100 g (3½ oz) low fat spread

1 egg

250 g (9 oz) chunky apple sauce
    (from a jar)

150 g (5½ oz) self-raising flour

1 teaspoon baking powder

1 teaspoon ground cinnamon

40 g (1½ oz) dried cranberries, chopped

2 apples, cored and sliced thinly

1   Preheat the oven to Gas Mark 4/180°C/fan oven 160°C. Line a rectangular baking tin measuring about 19 x 23 cm (7½ x 9 inches) with baking parchment.

2   Reserve ½ teaspoon caster sugar for the top of the cake. Beat the rest of the sugar and the low fat spread together until creamy, using an electric whisk or by hand. Add the egg and the apple sauce and beat again.

3   Sift in the flour, baking powder and cinnamon and mix well. Stir in the dried cranberries then smooth the cake mixture into the prepared cake tin.

4   Arrange the sliced apples on top of the cake, in four rows. Sprinkle with the reserved sugar then bake in the oven for 25–30 minutes until risen and firm in the centre. A skewer inserted into the centre of the cake should come out clean.

5   Cool the cake in the tin for 15 minutes then turn out on to a wire rack to finish cooling. Cut into 16 squares to serve, and store in an airtight tin for up to a couple of days, or freeze, well wrapped and labelled.

Cook's tip

To line a rectangular or square cake tin with baking parchment, turn the tin over and cut a piece of parchment so there is an extra 5 cm (2 inches) or so on each of the four sides. Fold in the sides so the paper fits the base neatly, then snip the paper at the corners so it fits easily inside the tin.

Together, the two fruits in this crumble create a gorgeous ruby red result and, as it cooks, an amazing aroma. This recipe is a great way to bring out the flavour of slightly under-ripe berries.

Rhubarb and strawberry crumble

Calories per serving 237

10 minutes preparation

35 minutes cooking

V Serves 4

250 g (9 oz) rhubarb, chopped roughly

40 g (1½ oz) caster sugar

75 g (2¾ oz) plain flour

40 g (1½ oz) low fat spread

40 g (1½ oz) soft light brown sugar

25 g (1 oz) porridge oats

250 g (9 oz) strawberries, trimmed
    and halved

1 Preheat the oven to Gas Mark 4/180°C/fan oven 160°C.

2 Put the rhubarb in a 20 cm (8 inch) square baking dish and toss with the caster sugar to coat. Bake for 10 minutes until the rhubarb is starting to look juicy.

3 Sift the flour into a mixing bowl then use your fingertips to rub the low fat spread in, until the mixture looks like breadcrumbs. Stir in the brown sugar and porridge oats.

4 Gently mix the strawberries in with the rhubarb then press the crumble topping on to the fruit.

5 Place on a baking tray and cook in the oven for 25 minutes or until the crumble is golden brown and crisp on top, with the scarlet juices from the fruit starting to bubble up around the edges.

Be sure to bake the rhubarb until its juices start to run and only then add the strawberries and crumble topping.

These scrumptious little custard tarts are great to serve at a party or as part of a buffet. Serve with fresh raspberries and blueberries.

Portuguese custard tarts

Calories per serving 95

20 minutes preparation

20 minutes cooking

V Makes 12

50 g (1¾ oz) caster sugar

1 tablespoon cornflour

1 egg

1 egg yolk

300 ml (10 fl oz) skimmed milk

2 teaspoons vanilla extract

2 teaspoons plain flour, for dusting

150 g (5½ oz) puff pastry

1 Preheat the oven to Gas Mark 7/220°C/fan oven 200°C.

2 Reserve 1 teaspoon of sugar for the top of the custard tarts then place the remainder in a non stick saucepan and add the cornflour, the whole egg and egg yolk. Stir until smooth then gradually blend in the milk.

3 Cook the mixture, stirring until it thickens and comes to the boil. Simmer for 1 minute then remove from the heat and add the vanilla. Sit the pan in a sink of cold water (to come no more than halfway up the pan) and leave to cool, stirring occasionally, while you prepare the tart cases.

4 Dust the work surface with a little of the flour. Roll the pastry out to a long thin rectangle measuring 12 x 25 cm (4½ x 10 inches). Roll up like a Swiss roll from the short end then slice into twelve 1 cm (½ inch) rounds.

5 Dust each pastry slice with a little flour and then roll out thinly to a circle measuring about 10 cm (4 inches) diameter – it doesn't matter if the circles are a bit uneven, it just adds to the rustic look. Press into a non stick 12-hole muffin tin, so that each muffin hole is lined.

6 Spoon the cooled custard into the pastry cases and sprinkle lightly with the reserved sugar.

7 Bake for 20 minutes or until the pastry is golden and the custard is caramelised in spots on top. Cool in the tin for 5 minutes before transferring to a wire rack to finish cooling.

Try this

For a slightly different flavour, add ½ teaspoon of ground cinnamon to the sugar before you sprinkle it on top of the custard tarts before baking.

These caramelised baked apples are ever so quick to prepare and superbly comforting to eat – it's the kind of recipe you find yourself cooking over and over again. Serve with a 60 g (2 oz) scoop of light vanilla ice cream, to give a deliciously hot and cold contrast.

Cinnamon and cider baked apples

Calories per serving 118

5 minutes preparation

25 minutes cooking

V Serves 2

2 teaspoons low fat spread

4 teaspoons light brown sugar

2 eating apples, halved

a pinch of ground cinnamon

100 ml (3½ fl oz) cider

1   Preheat the oven to Gas Mark 4/180°C/fan oven 160°C.

2   Melt the spread and sugar together in a non stick frying pan. Use a teaspoon to neatly scoop the central core out from each apple half then add to the frying pan, cut side down, and cook for 2 minutes over a high heat.

3   Sprinkle in the cinnamon then turn the apples over to coat in the syrupy juices before transferring to a small baking dish.

4   Add the cider to the frying pan and stir to release any sticky caramel from the base. Pour the cider over the apples in their baking dish and bake for 25 minutes or until tender and slightly puffy.

5   Cool slightly before serving, with the cooking juices spooned over.

Try this

Replace the apples with two halved pears.

A tea-time classic, this recipe illustrates just how easy it is to make a sponge cake yourself. You can easily vary the flavours; replacing the strawberry jam with lemon curd and the strawberries with blueberries is one possibility; or try flavouring the sponge with a few drops of almond extract instead of orange zest and use reduced sugar apricot jam and canned apricots to replace the strawberries and jam.

Strawberry sponge layer cake

Calories per serving 170

15 minutes preparation

20 minutes cooking

V ✳ for unfilled sponge only

Serves 10

100 g (3½ oz) self-raising flour

1 teaspoon baking powder

100 g (3½ oz) caster sugar

100 g (3½ oz) low fat spread

2 eggs

grated zest of ½ a small orange

50 g (1¾ oz) low fat soft cheese

2 teaspoons icing sugar

150 g (5½ oz) strawberries,
    trimmed and sliced

4 teaspoons reduced sugar
    strawberry jam

1   Preheat the oven to Gas Mark 4/180°C/fan oven 160°C. Line two 18 cm (7 inches) diameter sponge cake tins with baking parchment.

2   Sift the flour and baking powder into a mixing bowl, add the sugar, low fat spread, eggs and half the orange zest. Beat with a wooden spoon or an electric whisk, or by hand, for 2 minutes or until the cake mixture is pale and fluffy. Divide between the two sponge tins and spread out evenly.

3   Bake on the centre shelf of the oven for 15–18 minutes until the sponges are risen, golden brown and feel springy in the centre. The sponge should also be starting to pull away from the edges of the tin.

4   Cool on a wire rack for a few minutes then turn out of the tins, remove the lining parchment and leave to cool completely.

5   For the filling, beat the soft cheese with the rest of the orange zest plus 1½ teaspoons of icing sugar. Spread over the underside of one of the sponge layers and place on a serving plate. Top with the sliced strawberries (reserve a few slices for decoration if you wish).

6   Spread the jam on the underside of the second sponge layer then place this on top of the strawberries to sandwich the layers together. Dust the top of the cake with ½ teaspoon icing sugar just before serving, decorating with the reserved strawberry slices if desired.

Try this

For vanilla iced cupcakes: make the sponge mixture above (without the jam or strawberries) but replace the orange zest with 1 teaspoon vanilla extract. Divide between 12 paper cases in a bun tin and bake for 12–15 minutes until firm and springy.

For the icing: beat together 75 g (2¾ oz) low fat soft cheese, ½ teaspoon vanilla extract and 1½ teaspoons of sifted icing sugar until smooth. Spread over cooled cupcakes.

If you've got fruit that just won't seem to ripen up in the fruit bowl, this is a great way to turn it into something utterly delicious. You can make a larger batch if you wish, as the poached fruits keep well in their blush-pink syrup for a couple of days.

Vanilla poached fruits

Calories per serving 172

20 minutes in total + cooling + chilling

V Serves 2

40 g (1½ oz) caster sugar

300 ml (10 fl oz) boiling water

½ a lemon

½ a vanilla pod, split lengthways

1 pear, peeled, cored and cut into
    6 wedges

1 nectarine, stoned and cut into 6 wedges

2 plums, stoned and quartered

1 In a medium saucepan, dissolve the sugar in the boiling water. Remove two strips of zest from the lemon using a vegetable peeler (making sure that there is no bitter white pith attached) and add to the pan. Squeeze the juice from the half lemon and add that to the pan too, plus the split vanilla pod. Bring to the boil and simmer for 5 minutes to bring out the flavours.

2 Add the pear wedges first of all, and cook gently for 5 minutes (less if the pear is quite ripe). Then add the nectarine and plums and simmer for a further 5 minutes. Turn the fruit occasionally in the syrup so that it cooks evenly. When the fruit is tender, remove to a shallow dish and leave to cool.

3 Boil the syrup rapidly for 6–7 minutes or until reduced by half. Cool then pour over the cooled fruits. Chill until ready to serve.

Try this

You can vary the fruit in this recipe to suit, simply make sure that you poach the firmer, more densely textured fruit for longer than those with a naturally softer texture. You can even add fruits such as grapes or berries; these won't need poaching at all, simply mix them in with the flavoured syrup before the mixture is chilled.

Here's an ideal make-ahead dessert – it only takes 10 minutes to prepare then leave it to chill until ready to serve. It has a delicate flavour, full of lovely autumnal tastes.

Hedgerow jellies

Calories per serving 124

10 minutes preparation

    + cooling + chilling

Serves 4

4 sheets leaf gelatine

500 ml (18 fl oz) clear apple juice

juice of ½ a lemon

1 cinnamon stick

50 g (1¾ oz) caster sugar

150 g (5½ oz) blackberries

1   Place the sheets of gelatine in sufficient cold water to cover, and leave to soak and soften for 5 minutes.

2   Meanwhile, place the apple juice, lemon juice, cinnamon stick and sugar in a saucepan. Heat gently, stirring until the sugar dissolves, then simmer for 2 minutes. Remove from the heat.

3   Lift the softened gelatine out of the water and squeeze to remove the excess water. Add to the hot spiced apple juice and stir. The gelatine will dissolve almost immediately. Leave the liquid to cool then remove the cinnamon stick.

4   Divide the blackberries between four glasses or ramekins then pour the jelly mixture on top.

5   Cover with cling film and chill in the fridge for 2 hours or until firm.

Cook's tips

Leaf gelatine is the easiest form of gelatine to use, as it dissolves so easily. However, you can substitute with powdered gelatine if you prefer. There's no need to soak powdered gelatine, simply sprinkle the powder over the hot spiced apple juice at the end of step 2, stirring all the time until it has dissolved. Continue as above.

If you want to speed up the cooling process, stand the pan in a large bowl of cold water (making sure that it isn't too full, as you don't want to get any water inside the pan). Stir occasionally as it cools.

These lovely little puddings are inspired by the exotic flavours of Middle Eastern cuisine, but given a lift with a hint of dark rum.

Rum baba puddings
with mandarins and pistachio

Calories per serving 305

10 minutes preparation

15 minutes cooking

V Serves 6

calorie controlled cooking spray

*2 x 298 g cans mandarin segments
    in natural juice*

1 tablespoon dark rum

100 g (3½ oz) caster sugar

100 g (3½ oz) low fat spread

100 g (3½ oz) self-raising flour

½ teaspoon baking powder

2 eggs

grated zest of ½ an orange

*15 g (½ oz) shelled unsalted pistachios,
    chopped finely*

1   Preheat the oven to Gas Mark 4/180°C/fan oven 160°C. Lightly spray six sections of a muffin tray with the cooking spray.

2   Drain the juice from the can of mandarin segments and set the fruit aside. Pour the juice into a saucepan, bring to the boil and simmer briskly for 10 minutes or until reduced by half and slightly syrupy. Add the rum and set aside.

3   Meanwhile, to make the puddings, using an electric whisk, beat the sugar with the low fat spread, flour, baking powder, eggs and grated orange zest in a mixing boil until pale and creamy. Stir in the pistachios then spoon into the prepared muffin tray. Bake in the oven for 15 minutes, or until the puddings are risen, golden and firm to the touch.

4   Turn the puddings out on to a deep plate or shallow dish. Spoon the rum syrup over the warm puddings to soak in. Serve with the drained mandarin segments.

Coffee offers a fabulous flavour twist to classic crème caramels. They also have a lovely smooth consistency, thanks to the gentle baking in a hot water bath.

Coffee crème caramel

Calories per serving 193

15 minutes preparation + cooling

20 minutes cooking

V Serves 6

150 g (5½ oz) granulated sugar

a kettleful of boiling water

500 ml (18 fl oz) skimmed milk

4 eggs

1 teaspoon vanilla extract

2 teaspoons instant coffee dissolved
  in 1 tablespoon boiling water

1 Preheat the oven to Gas Mark 2/150°C/fan oven 130°C.

2   To make the caramel, place 100 g (3½ oz) of the sugar in a saucepan with 4 tablespoons boiling water. Heat gently, stirring, until the sugar has completely dissolved.

3 Increase the heat under the pan and boil the syrup for about 5 minutes or until it is a rich golden brown. Don't stir (as it may cause the syrup to crystallise and solidify); instead, shake the pan occasionally.

4 Pour the syrup into six 150 ml (5 fl oz) ramekins and swirl to coat the base of each.

5 Add the milk and the remaining sugar to the syrup pan. Bring to a simmer.

6 Meanwhile, whisk the eggs and vanilla together in a bowl then add the hot milk and the dissolved coffee.

7 Place the ramekins in a large roasting tin then add boiling water to come halfway up the outside of the ramekins.

8 Strain the egg mixture into the ramekins, pouring it through a tea strainer or sieve to catch any eggy threads.

9 Bake in the oven until the crème caramels feel just firm to the touch when the centre is pressed gently. Use a turner or wooden spatula to lift the ramekins out of their hot water bath and transfer to a wire rack to cool. Once cool, chill in the fridge for at least an hour.

10 To serve, run a knife around the edge of each ramekin to release. Place a plate on top then swiftly turn the plate and ramekin upside down, giving them a shake to loosen the crème caramel from its mould.

Cook's tips

The crème caramels are baked in a hot water bath (also known as a bain marie) to give them a lovely smooth texture. Because the water can't rise above 100°C, it keeps a steady temperature so they can't overheat and curdle as they bake.

If there are any lumps of caramel stuck to the saucepan, simply add water and bring to the boil to dissolve them. This is much more effective than trying to scrub them off.

Attractive to the eye, and to the palate, these marbled meringues deliver an intense chocolatey hit. Simply scrumptious.

Marbled meringues with chocolate mousse

Calories per serving 190

20 minutes preparation

40 minutes cooking

V Serves 6

2 egg whites

100 g (3½ oz) caster sugar

1 heaped teaspoon cocoa powder

75 g (2¾ oz) dark chocolate with 75% cocoa solids

2 heaped teaspoons clear honey

150 g (5½ oz) Quark, at room temperature

400 g (14 oz) strawberries, sliced

1 Preheat the oven to Gas Mark 2/150°C/fan oven 130°C and line a large baking tray with baking parchment.

2 Place the egg whites in a perfectly clean bowl (there must be no trace of fat on the bowl or on your whisk, otherwise they won't beat up into a froth). Use an electric whisk or hand held whisk to beat the egg whites. If using an electric whisk, start on a low speed until the egg whites look quite frothy, then gradually increase the speed. Starting out on a low speed means that lots of tiny bubbles are formed rather than fewer large bubbles, giving a more stable structure to your meringues.

3 Continue to beat until the egg whites reach the stiff peak stage. Lift the whisk out of the egg whites and turn it upside down; if they have reached stiff peak stage then the tip will stand up straight.

4 Gradually add the sugar to the beaten egg whites, a spoonful at a time, beating well between each addition until you have a stiff, shiny meringue mixture. Transfer a large spoonful of the meringue to another bowl then fold in the cocoa powder. Add the chocolate meringue to the rest of the meringue. Gently fold together until lightly marbled.

5 Spoon the meringue into six mounds on the prepared baking tray. Use the back of a spoon to gently hollow out the centre of each mound, making a meringue nest about 8 cm (3¼ inches) in diameter. Bake in the oven for 40 minutes until the meringues feel crisp, and can easily be peeled from the parchment. Turn off the oven, but leave the meringues in it as it cools. The cooled meringues can be stored in an airtight container for a couple of weeks.

6 To make the chocolate mousse, break up the chocolate and place in a heatproof bowl. Sit the bowl on top of a small pan with 2.5 cm (1 inch) depth of gently simmering, not boiling, water, making sure that the bottom of the bowl doesn't touch the water. Heat for 2–3 minutes until the chocolate has melted then remove the bowl and leave the chocolate to cool to room temperature.

7 Stir first the honey, and then the Quark into the melted chocolate, mixing well until smooth. The mixture will thicken almost immediately. The mousse can be served straightaway, or kept at room temperature for up to an hour. Otherwise, cover and refrigerate until ready to use, but return to room temperature to soften before use. Divide the chocolate mousse between the meringue nests and spoon the strawberries on top.

This Italian-inspired dessert is a great choice for a supper party – you're sure to get plenty of compliments. It's also great for a buffet as it's make-ahead and is so easy to slice into individual portions.

Berry tiramisu with white chocolate

Calories per serving 194

20 minutes + chilling

V Serves 8

350 g (12 oz) frozen summer fruits

50 g (1¾ oz) caster sugar

1 tablespoon brandy (optional)

250 g (9 oz) Quark

200 g (7 oz) virtually fat-free plain
    fromage frais

1 teaspoon vanilla extract

2 tablespoons icing sugar

24 sponge fingers

50 g (1¾ oz) white chocolate, grated finely

1 Line a 900 g (2 lb) loaf tin with cling film – it helps to dampen the inside of the tin first so that the cling film will stick to the sides.

2 Place the summer fruits in a lidded saucepan with the caster sugar and 3 tablespoons of water. Cook, covered, for 4–5 minutes until the fruits have defrosted and are juicy, but don't bring to the boil. Tip the fruits into a sieve over a bowl to catch the juice. If using, add the brandy to the juice. Set the fruits and juice aside.

3 In a mixing bowl, beat together the Quark, fromage frais, vanilla extract and icing sugar until smooth.

4 Dip eight of the sponge fingers into the fruit juice, leaving to soak for a few seconds, but not for too long or they will soften and fall apart. Arrange in the bottom of the lined loaf tin.

5 Spoon half of the Quark mixture on top of the sponge fingers then add a third of the grated white chocolate and half of the summer fruits. Add another layer of fruit-dipped sponge fingers, Quark mixture, chocolate and summer fruits. Finish with the rest of the sponge fingers, once again dipping them in the juice.

6 Cover with cling film and cut a piece of card to fit just inside the top of the loaf tin. Weight down with a couple of tin cans then chill in the fridge for 4 hours.

7 Carefully turn out the tiramisu on to a serving plate and remove the cling film. Scatter the rest of the white chocolate on top then cut into eight slices.

As unbelievable as it might seem, although made from scratch, these magnificent little sponge puddings can be on the table in just 10 minutes as they are cooked in the microwave, giving them a lovely light texture.

Speedy syrup sponges

Calories per serving 199
10 minutes in total
V Serves 4

calorie controlled cooking spray
4 level teaspoons golden syrup
1 egg
50 g (1¾ oz) low fat spread
60 g (2 oz) self-raising flour
50 g (1¾ oz) caster sugar
1 tablespoon skimmed milk

1 Lightly spray four microwaveable mini pudding basins with cooking spray. Measure 1 level teaspoon of golden syrup into the base of each one.

2 Place the egg, low fat spread, flour, caster sugar and milk in a mixing bowl and beat with an electric whisk, or a hand whisk, until pale and fluffy. Divide between the pudding basins. It won't come very far up, but the puddings will rise considerably during cooking.

3 Cover each pudding basin in cling film; the speediest way to do this is to set out the pudding basins like the four corners of a square, leaving space between them, and then stretch a single piece of cling film over the top. Use kitchen scissors to cut between the basins and loosely tuck the cling film over the sides of each basin. This is much less fiddly than cutting individual pieces of cling film to size. Pierce a hole in the top of each piece of cling film.

4 Place the puddings in the microwave and cook for 2½ minutes at 800W. Leave to stand for 1 minute then turn out the puddings and serve.

Try this
If you like custard with your syrup sponge, serve each one with ½ x 135 g pot of low fat custard.

When you need a chocolate lift, these gorgeous chocolate cherry cupcakes will certainly hit the spot, and feel like a real indulgence.

Chocolate cherry cupcakes

Calories per serving 145
20 minutes preparation
20 minutes cooking
V ✳ minus fresh cherry garnish
Makes 12

175 g (6 oz) fresh cherries
25 g (1 oz) cocoa, sifted
150 g (5½ oz) self-raising flour
1 teaspoon bicarbonate of soda
100 g (3½ oz) dark brown sugar
75 g (2¾ oz) low fat spread
1 egg
1 teaspoon vanilla extract
150 g (5½ oz) virtually fat-free
    natural yogurt
100 g (3½ oz) low fat soft cheese
15 g (½ oz) icing sugar, sifted

1   Preheat the oven to Gas Mark 4/180°C/fan oven 160°C and line a 12 hole muffin tin with paper cases.

2   Start by stoning the cherries; if you have an olive pitter, this works really well on cherries too. Otherwise, place the cherries on a chopping board and roll over them with a rolling pin to crush them lightly, then squeeze out the stones. Reserve six cherries, halved, to decorate then chop up the rest of the cherries roughly.

3   Reserve 2 teaspoons of the cocoa to make the frosting, then sift the rest of the cocoa, the flour and the bicarbonate of soda into a mixing bowl. Add the sugar, low fat spread, egg, vanilla and yogurt and beat together with an electric whisk, or hand held whisk, until light and fluffy. Stir the chopped cherries into the mixture then divide between the paper cake cases.

4   Bake on the centre shelf of the oven for 15–18 minutes until the cupcakes are well risen and feel springy in the centre.

5   Remove to a wire rack to cool.

6   For the frosting, beat the cheese together with the icing sugar and the reserved cocoa. Spread on to the cooled cupcakes then top each one with a half cherry to serve.

Cheat's tip
If you want to skip stoning fresh cherries (or they are too expensive because they are out of season), then use a 425 g can cherries in natural juice, drained and patted dry on kitchen paper.

Glossary

Al dente: an Italian term that translates literally as 'to the tooth', often used for pasta, meaning to cook until the pasta is tender but still retains a little bite, rather than being completely soft.

Bake blind: to bake a pastry case for a quiche or flan while empty. In order to prevent the sides from falling in or the base bubbling up, the pastry is usually lined with baking parchment and filled with 'baking beans'.

Baking beans: dried beans, ceramic baking beans, peas, rice or pasta used to temporarily fill pastry cases during blind baking (can be re-used for further blind baking, but not as an ingredient).

Bain-marie: a piece of equipment used to heat things gradually at a certain temperature or keep them warm. An example is a baking tin half-filled with hot water in which egg custards and similar dishes stand while cooking, to regulate the temperature and prevent over-heating.

Beat: to combine ingredients together with a whisk or wooden spoon until they are smooth (see also 'whisk').

Blanch: to parboil vegetables so that they are lightly cooked, then 'refreshed', ready for reheating before serving.

Braise: to bake or stew meat slowly on a bed of vegetables, in a lidded casserole or dish.

Brown: to cook ingredients over a high heat until they turn brown. Care must be taken not to overcrowd the pan.

Caramelise: to cook an ingredient until the natural sugars in it are released and turned to caramel (in other words, when it turns brown).

Chop: finely chopping an ingredient implies a size of 0.5 cm–1 cm pieces. Roughly chopping may be any size larger than this (see also 'dice').

Coat: to cover in a coating, for example: flour, egg and breadcrumbs.

Cooling rack: usually a simple wire rack on which baked goods are cooled, turned out of their tins. This allows air to circulate all around so that the underside doesn't become soggy.

Coulis: a thick, smooth-textured sauce

Cream: to beat ingredients together such as sugar and fat when making a sponge cake.

Deglaze: to loosen the fat, sediment and browned juices stuck on the bottom of a frying pan or saucepan, by adding liquid (such as water, wine or stock) and stirring while boiling.

De-seed: to remove the seeds e.g. from peppers, chillies, tomatoes.

Dice: to cut food into tiny squares (e.g. a carrot), approx 2–3 mm.

Dropping consistency: the consistency when a mixture will drop reluctantly from a spoon, neither running off nor obstinately adhering. Often used to refer to the correct consistency of a cake mixture.

Dust: to sprinkle with either flour or icing sugar, usually through a sieve or strainer.

Egg wash: beaten raw egg, sometimes with a pinch of salt added for an even shinier result, used for glazing pastry to give it a shine when baked.

Fold: to mix with a gentle lifting motion, rather than stirring vigorously, when you want to avoid knocking the air out of a mixture while combining ingredients.

Glaze: to cover with a shiny coating. This might be a thin layer of melted jam for fruit flans and desserts, syrup or thin icing on a sponge, egg wash on a pastry pie topping, or jellied meat juices for roasted meat.

Infuse: to gently heat a liquid (e.g. milk) with flavourings, such as onion.

Julienne: a chef's term for vegetables cut into very thin shreds or matchsticks.

Knock down or knock back: punching or kneading the air out of risen dough, before shaping, proving and baking.

Marinade: a mixture of flavouring ingredients, generally containing an acidic ingredient such as lemon juice or yogurt, which adds flavour to (usually) meat and helps to tenderise it. The meat is marinated in the marinade.

Oven to tableware: baking dishes and casseroles with an attractive appearance which means they can be used to serve from at the table without looking too utilitarian.

Papillote: a paper parcel in which fish or meat is cooked, to contain the aroma and flavour (foil can also be used).

Parboil: to half-boil or partially soften by boiling

Pass: to strain or push through a sieve

Pinch: the amount of an ingredient that can be held between the thumb and fingers is known as a pinch ie. a pinch of salt

Poussin: baby chicken

Preheat: an oven will take a while to reach the desired temperature after being turned on, so it's wise to turn it on when you start to prepare your food, to give it time to preheat.

Prove: to leave shaped dough to rise before baking

Purée: liquidised or sieved fruit or vegetables

Reduce: to reduce the amount of liquid by rapid boiling. Evaporation concentrates the flavour in the remaining liquid.

Refresh: to stop the cooking process of (usually) green vegetables by holding them under the cold tap. This also sets their colour.

Relax or rest: to set pastry aside in a cool place such as the fridge to allow the gluten (which will have stretched during rolling), to contract. This reduces the risk of pastry shrinking in the oven.

Return to boil: when you add an ingredient to a saucepan of already boiling water, you then need to bring the water back to the boil. Cooking times are calculated from when the water has returned to the boil.

Rubbing in fat: a technique where you rub fat and flour together between your fingers, lifting your hands up and allowing the mixture to fall back into the bowl, until the mixture looks like breadcrumbs.

Sauté: to fry on the hob, while tossing or shaking the pan, so that the food browns quickly and evenly.

Sear/seal: to brown pieces of meat rapidly for colour and flavour.

Sift: to shake e.g. flour through a sieve into a bowl, incorporating air and eliminating lumps.

Slake: to mix cornflour (or arrowroot/flour/custard powder) to a thin paste with a little cold water

Slice: 'finely sliced' implies slices about 2–3 mm thick, sliced about 5 mm thick, while thickly sliced is 1 cm or more.

Soft peak/stiff peak: particularly used with regard to meringue mixture. Dip your whisk into the mixture then turn it upright. If the peak flops to the side, it is at soft peak stage, but if it holds up, it is at stiff peak stage.

Spice rub: a mixture of dry spices (often bought ready-made), which is rubbed into raw meat, poultry or fish before cooking to add flavour and colour.

Stir-fry: to briskly fry finely chopped and sliced ingredients over a high heat, while stirring, to cook them quickly. Always make sure that all your ingredients are prepared before you start stir-frying as the cooking process is so quick.

Steam-fry: as for stir-fry, but adding some water to the pan near the end of the cooking time to ensure that the ingredients cook through.

Stock powder: a useful alternative to stock cubes, especially for making small amounts of stock. Stock made from powder generally has a less overpowering flavour than that made from a cube. As a rule of thumb, use 1 teaspoon stock powder to make 300 ml (10 fl oz) stock.

Sustainable fish: fish (or seafood) which come from well-managed sources and/or are caught using methods that minimise damage to marine wildlife and habitats.

Sweat: to cook gently, usually in butter or oil, or in the food's own juices or a little stock, without frying or browning, until softened.

Thicken: to add a thickening agent such as 'slaked' cornflour or flour to a sauce that is too thin.

Translucent: slightly see-through e.g. when a chopped or sliced onion is cooked, it will change from being white and opaque to being translucent.

Whisk: to beat air into a mixture until it is light and fluffy

Yeast: can be bought fresh or dried, with the most common type being active dried yeast which can be added straight to flour in its dry state. An opened part-used package can be re-sealed and kept for up to one month in dry surroundings (moisture will reduce its effectiveness).

Zest: the thin coloured skin of an orange, lemon or lime, used to add concentrated flavour. Generally used grated, but may also be pared using a vegetable peeler, in which case ensure that none of the bitter white pith is attached. Always wash and scrub citrus fruit before removing the zest, to get rid of any wax coating that has been added in the production process.

Index